The CALL of GRACE

The CALL of GRACE

How the Covenant
Illuminates Salvation
and Evangelism

NORMAN SHEPHERD

P&R

PUBLISHING
P.O. BOX 817 • PHILLIPSBURG • NEW JERSEY 08865-0817

Scripture quotations are from the HOLY BIBLE, NEW INTERNATIONAL VERSION®. NIV®. Copyright © 1973, 1978, 1984 by International Bible Society. Used by permission of Zondervan Publishing House. All rights reserved.

Italics in Bible quotations indicate emphasis added.

Page design by Tobias Design
Typesetting by Michelle Feaster

Printed in the United States of America

Library of Congress Cataloging-in-Publication Data

Shepherd, Norman, 1933–
    The call of grace : how the covenant illuminates salvation and evangelism / Norman Shepherd.
        p.   cm.
    Includes index.
    ISBN 0-87552-459-1 (pbk.)
    1. Salvation. 2. Evangelistic work—Philosophy. 3. Covenant theology. I. Title.

BT751.2 S515 2000
231.7'6—dc21

                                            00-055809

Contents

Preface

What distinguishes the Reformed faith from all the other confessional options found among sincere Christians? This question is usually answered by reference to the five points of Calvinism as defined by the Synod of Dordt in 1619. These points are total depravity, unconditional election, limited or definite atonement, irresistible grace, and perseverance of the saints. They make clear that when it comes to salvation from sin and eternal condemnation, the sinner is wholly unable to help himself. God alone determines whom he will save, and actually saves them for eternity.

While these doctrines are certainly characteristic of, and indispensable to, full-orbed Calvinism, they do not do full justice to the uniqueness of Calvinism as a system of doctrine and as a world-and-life view. In my own study of God's word, I have come to appreciate the Reformed emphases on covenant and kingdom as the leading and distinguishing characteristics of the Reformed faith. No other confessional grouping has given nearly the same attention to biblical teaching in these areas.

The biblical teaching on covenant in particular is especially helpful in dealing with certain issues that have arisen just because of our adherence to the five points. The Reformed faith makes clear that salvation is all of divine grace from beginning to end. But if that is so, where and how does human responsibility enter in? The presentations that follow are an attempt to shed light on two separate but related aspects of that question from the perspective of covenant.

The first part deals with the problem of faith and works, or grace and merit. This issue has come to the fore once again in recent discussions between evangelical Protestants and Roman Catholics, as well as among evangelicals themselves. The material for this part was developed for the Robinson Lectures at Erskine Theological Seminary in Due West, South Carolina, and presented on April 14 and 15, 1999. I would like to express my appreciation to the dean, Dr. R. J. Gore, and to the faculty of Erskine Seminary for the kind invitation to take part in this lectureship established in memory of Richard Lee Robinson, dean of the seminary from 1933 to 1939. The three lectures in the series are presented here with only minor revisions.

The second part deals with a perennial issue faced by Calvinists who take seriously the call to evangelize the lost with a view to their conversion to Christ and salvation in him. If God is sovereign in the planning, accomplishment, and application of redemption, how can we honestly and sincerely call sinners to faith and tell them to repent, without compromising the five points? The material for this part was originally presented at a presynodical conference sponsored by the Reformed Presbyterian Church of North America at Geneva College in Beaver Falls, Pennsylvania, on May 19, 1975. It was subsequently published in *The New Testament Student and Theology,* edited by John H. Skilton (Presbyterian and Reformed, 1976). Because of continuing interest in the perspective developed in this article, it is offered here in a revised form.

It is my sincere hope that the biblical teaching on covenant will serve to shed light on some otherwise perplexing issues concerning the all-important topics of evangelism and the way of salvation.

PART 1

Covenant Light on the Way of Salvation

FACING A NEW CHALLENGE

On the threshold of a new century and a new millennium, we are painfully aware of the challenge of secularization. Christian principles and standards of behavior are increasingly excluded from the public domain, and morality appears to be in a free fall. Christianity is being challenged, not only by an aggressive secularism, but also by pantheism through the New Age movement, and by a militant Islamic faith. Many believe that we are living in a post-Christian era. In the face of this, Christians sense the need to band together to offer resistance. They sense the need to maintain a clear testimony against unbelief, immorality, and social disintegration.

One attempt to meet this challenge resulted in a declaration published in 1994 entitled *Evangelicals and Catholics Together*. This document was designed to explain and celebrate "a pattern of convergence and cooperation" between evangelical Protestants and Roman Catholics. Charles Colson, chairman of Prison Fellowship Ministries and one of the initiators of this project, said, "We have differences, but on the ancient creeds and the core beliefs of Christianity we stand together."

This declaration met with a broad measure of support in the evangelical community, but it also met with some strong criticism. As a result of this criticism, a second document was published with the title *The Gift of Salvation*. It was designed to address certain perceived ambiguities in the first document. One of these areas had to do with the way of salvation and the doctrine of justification by faith.

This second document also met with mixed reaction. Some evangelical scholars gave it "cautious support." Others sounded the alarm and warned that basic principles of the Protestant Reformation were being surrendered. This negative assessment found expression in a document produced by the Alliance of Confessing Evangelicals called *An Appeal to Fellow Evangelicals*. Other exchanges have followed, and in an attempt to reconcile differences a "call to evangelical unity" was issued in the summer of 1999 in the form of a document with the title *The Gospel of Jesus Christ: An Evangelical Celebration*. Signatories to this statement include evangelical scholars on both sides of the *Evangelicals and Catholics Together* debate.

FACING AN OLD PROBLEM

It is not my purpose to discuss the details of these documents or to explore the nuances of this debate. We simply note the significance of this discussion. It is another indication of some unresolved questions that are really the legacy of the Protestant Reformation.

During the centuries leading up to the Reformation, salvation from sin and eternal condemnation came to be seen as a reward for good works. With help from the church and the sacramental system, a sinner could become a righteous person, and by his good works he could merit eternal life.

It was this teaching that caused Martin Luther so much grief and anxiety. He could never be sure that he was good enough to inherit eternal life. His sins condemned him, and he faced death with no assurance of salvation.

Through his reading and study of God's word, Luther came to see that salvation was by grace alone through faith alone. Because of what Jesus had done during his life and in his death on the cross, sinners could be saved by receiving him in faith. We are saved by grace through faith. We are not saved by good works through merit.

This doctrine has brought great comfort to God's people. It is a doctrine that points us to grace that is greater than all our sin. What we could never do for ourselves because of our sinful nature, Christ has done for us.

We are profoundly grateful for the progress that was made by the Reformation. We were led into a more biblical understanding of the way of salvation. Nonetheless, unresolved issues remain. There have been long-standing differences between adherents of the historic Lutheran and Reformed confessions. That is evident especially in their different attitudes toward the law. The law can serve to reveal and convince us of our sin, but Lutherans fear that making the commandments a rule for Christian living will confuse law and gospel. They fear that it will confuse salvation by grace with salvation by works.

Differences surfaced among the Reformed in the Marrow controversy of the eighteenth century. More recently, differences among evangelicals have surfaced in the controversy over lordship salvation. Now we have the discussions to which reference was made earlier. The *Appeal to Fellow Evangelicals* speaks of "severe controversy within the ranks of professing Evangelicals." It says, "The unity we thought we had was not as deep as we believed." The more recent call to evangelical unity does not seek to deal with some key

Scripture passages that played a significant role in earlier discussions. As these passages begin to assert themselves once more in the ongoing discussions, it may still be the case that "the unity we thought we had was not as deep as we believed."

What are these differences, and why are they so persistent and intractable? What is the root of the problem?

ANTINOMIANISM AND LEGALISM

The differences can be summarized as the differences between legalism and antinomianism. Children of the Reformation insist that salvation is by grace alone. There is nothing that you can do or should try to do to save yourself. For some, salvation by grace means that you make a decision for Christ. You believe in him and are saved. Of course, the commandments are important and Christians should be concerned about holy living. After all, Jesus said that "if you love me, you will obey what I command" (John 14:15). But all of that has nothing to do with your salvation or your eternal security. Salvation is by grace alone through faith alone. You receive Jesus as your Savior, but whether you receive him as Lord of your life is another matter. You *ought* to do that, but *whether* you do so will not affect your eternal destiny. Your eternal destiny has nothing to do with how you live your life, because you are not saved by works. If you have accepted Jesus as your Savior, that is all that matters as far as salvation is concerned.

We call this way of thinking "antinomian." The word means, literally, "against law." The term brings out the fact that law keeping plays no role in the way of salvation. The strength of antinomianism is its appeal to what is at the heart of the Protestant Reformation: salvation by grace though faith, not by merit through works.

Over against the antinomians, others point out that it isn't quite that simple. According to the teaching of James in the second chapter of his letter, faith without works is dead. Such faith is of no use. It will not save. James reflects the teaching of Jesus, who called sinners to repentance. Repentance is not only sorrow for sin, but also a turning away from sin. Jesus taught his disciples to preach repentance for the forgiveness of sins to all the nations (Luke 24:47). That is why Peter preached repentance on the Day of Pentecost (Acts 2). That is why Paul preached repentance on Mars Hill in Athens (Acts 17). When he defended himself before King Agrippa, Paul made the point that he preached repentance to both Jews and Gentiles. "I preached that they should repent and turn to God and prove their repentance by their deeds" (Acts 26:20). Paul wrote to the Galatians, "God cannot be mocked. A man reaps what he sows. The one who sows to please his sinful nature, from that nature will reap destruction; the one who sows to please the Spirit, from the Spirit will reap eternal life" (Gal. 6:7–8).

Most of us who belong to Reformed churches are comfortable with this way of speaking. It is obviously biblical, and it is what we confess, for example, in the Heidelberg Catechism. In Lord's Day 32, the question is, "Can those be saved who do not turn to God from their ungrateful and impenitent ways?" The answer is, "By no means. Scripture tells us that no unchaste person, no idolater, adulterer, thief, no covetous person, no drunkard, slanderer, robber, or the like is going to inherit the kingdom of God."

Many evangelicals, however, argue that if you preach repentance and press for the necessity of obedience, you are preaching legalism. Then you are on your way back to the Church of Rome and the doctrine of salvation by good works. This sentiment is embodied in a well-known hymn with these words:

> *Free from the law—O happy condition!*
> *Jesus hath bled, and there is remission;*
> *Cursed by the law and bruised by the fall,*
> *Grace hath redeemed us once and for all.*

Many understand this kind of language to mean freedom, not only from the *curse* of the law, but also from its *demands*. We are always being reminded that believers are not under law, but under grace!

What we have been looking at so far is the legacy of the Reformation on its downside. It is the controversy between antinomianism and legalism. It is the controversy between Rome and the Reformation. It is the historic difference between the Lutherans and the Reformed with respect to the use of the law. Many would even see it as the difference between the Old Testament, with its focus on law, and the New Testament, with its focus on grace. Within the compass of the Old Testament, it is construed as the difference between the covenant with Abraham and the covenant with Moses. That difference is the difference between promise and command, between promise and obligation.

This is a serious issue, with serious practical consequences for ministry and evangelism. The issue can be formulated by posing these questions: How do you preach *grace* without suggesting that it makes no difference what your lifestyle is like? In other words, how do you preach grace without being antinomian? On the other hand, how do you preach *repentance* without calling into question salvation by grace apart from works? How do you insist on obedience without being legalistic?

We can find the answers to these questions in the light of the biblical doctrine of covenant. We will begin by looking at the covenant that the Lord God made with Abraham. Then we will look successively at the Mosaic and the new covenants, before seeking to draw some conclusions.

The Bible does not leave us caught on the horns of a dilemma. Divine grace and human responsibility are not antithetical to each other. They are the two sides, or the two parts, of the covenant that God has made with us and with our children.

❦ 1

The Abrahamic Covenant

PROMISE IN THE ABRAHAMIC COVENANT

We begin with the Abrahamic covenant. The book of Genesis testifies that God made a covenant with Abraham and his children. Genesis 12:2–3 tells of the promise that God made to Abraham to make of him a great nation. Abraham would be a blessing, and through him all peoples on the earth would be blessed. The word *covenant* is not used in chapter 12, but it is used in Genesis 15:18: "On that day the LORD made a covenant with Abram and said, 'To your descendants I give this land, from the river of Egypt to the great river, the Euphrates.' "

It is especially in chapter 17, however, that we see the full scope of covenantal language:

> I will confirm my covenant between me and you and will greatly increase your numbers. (v. 2)

> I will establish my covenant as an everlasting
> covenant between me and you and your descen-
> dants after you for the generations to come, to be
> your God and the God of your descendants after
> you. The whole land of Canaan, where you are now
> an alien, I will give as an everlasting possession to
> you and your descendants after you; and I will be
> their God. (vv. 7–8)

The establishment of this covenant is one of the epochal
events of biblical history.

Before we proceed further, it will be useful to indicate
what the Bible means by *covenant*. Of course, there are
covenants that human beings make with one another. Our
concern at the moment, however, is with the covenant relationship that God has established with believers and their
children. It is a relationship that comes to expression in a
series of historical covenants. Two of these covenants are
the Abrahamic and the Mosaic. We can describe a covenant
as a divinely established relationship of union and communion between God and his people in the bonds of mutual love
and faithfulness. The biblical basis for this description will
become apparent as we proceed. In the Abrahamic
covenant, God entered into union and communion with
Abraham and his children, promising them his steadfast
love and requiring the same response from them.

Of special significance for us right now is the fact that
in this covenant God's promises to Abraham are in the foreground. In Genesis 12:3, the promise is that in and through
Abraham all the peoples on earth will be blessed. In Genesis 15, God promises children to Abraham even though he
and his wife have grown old. God "took him outside and

said, 'Look up at the heavens and count the stars—if indeed you can count them.' Then he said to him, 'So shall your offspring be'" (v. 5). God not only promises Abraham children, but also promises him a place for these children to live. "On that day the LORD made a covenant with Abram and said, 'To your descendants I give this land, from the river of Egypt to the great river, the Euphrates'" (vv. 18–20). God promises Abraham descendants and a place for them to live. In a dramatic ceremony described in verses 8–11 and 17, the Lord God commits himself to fulfill this promise, so that Abraham can be sure that he will gain possession of the Promised Land.

The heart of the promises made to Abraham is found in a verse already cited from Genesis 17: "I will establish my covenant as an everlasting covenant between me and you and your descendants after you for the generations to come, to be your God and the God of your descendants after you" (v. 7). God promises to be Abraham's God and the God of his children forever.

CONDITIONALITY IN THE ABRAHAMIC COVENANT

Frequently these promises made to Abraham are said to be *unconditional*. God has committed himself to fulfill them, irrespective of Abraham's response. There are no conditions attached to these promises that have to be met before they are realized. For example, one author comments on Genesis 22 that the Lord "now pledges himself on oath, and unconditionally, to do for Abraham all that he had originally promised."

Because the fulfillment of the promise is unconditional,

the Abrahamic covenant is viewed as a model for the method of gospel grace. There is nothing that you have to do to be saved; you are saved by grace alone. The Abrahamic covenant is then set over against the Mosaic covenant, thought of as a legalistic covenant, in which you are saved by keeping this republished covenant of works perfectly, without any exception. In this way, the Mosaic covenant serves as a proof text for legalism. At the same time, the Abrahamic covenant serves as a proof text for antinomianism.

But now we ought to ask whether the covenant that God made with Abraham really was, in fact, unconditional. Would the promises be fulfilled irrespective of any response on the part of Abraham and his children? The biblical record shows that conditions were, indeed, attached to the fulfillment of the promises made to Abraham. There are at least six considerations that serve to demonstrate this point.

1. There was the requirement of circumcision. God required Abraham and his children to keep the covenant by practicing circumcision (Gen. 17:9–14). If this was not done, the covenant was broken and the uncircumcised male was to be cut off from his people. Such a one would not inherit what was promised. Circumcision was clearly a condition for inheriting what was promised.

When God required circumcision as a condition in the Abrahamic covenant, his concern was not merely with an outward ceremony. This is clear from the prophecy of Jeremiah against Israelites who were circumcised only in the flesh, but not in their hearts (Jer. 4:4; 9:25). The apostle Paul alludes to this judgment when he writes in Romans 2:28, "A man is not a Jew if he is only one outwardly, nor is circumcision merely outward and physical." In requiring circumcision, God was requiring the full scope of covenantal loyalty and obedience all along the line. That was the significance of circumcision in the Abrahamic covenant.

We may note in passing that baptism has the same significance in the new covenant. In the Great Commission, Jesus teaches us to disciple the nations by baptizing them and teaching them to obey everything he has commanded. That is why one of the liturgical forms for the administration of baptism to infants used in Christian Reformed churches contains these words: "Third, because all covenants have two sides, baptism also places us under obligation to live in obedience to God." Baptism has come in the place of circumcision. Just as circumcision obliged Israel to obey God under the old covenant, so also baptism obliges believers to obey him under the new covenant.

2. The Abrahamic covenant required faith. It belongs to the very nature of promises that they cry out to be believed. Thus, the promises made to Abraham had to be believed if they were to be fulfilled. We must not discount faith as a condition to be met for the fulfillment of promise. In fact, Genesis 15:6 says that Abraham's faith was so significant that it was credited to him as righteousness! If so, then righteousness was a condition to be met, and faith met that condition.

3. The faith that was credited to Abraham as righteousness was a living and obedient faith. Hebrews 11 describes Abraham as a man of faith, but his faith was not a purely mental act. It was no armchair faith. By faith, Abraham obeyed the voice of God and left his homeland in order to inherit a Promised Land. By faith, he was ready to offer Isaac as a sacrifice, confident that God would nevertheless fulfill his promise.

James 2 is even more explicit. Verse 21 says that Abraham was considered righteous for what he did when he offered his son Isaac on the altar. His faith and his actions were working together, and his faith was made complete by what he did. Verse 23 says, "And the scripture was fulfilled that says, 'Abraham believed God, and it was credited to him as righteousness,' and he was called God's friend."

James goes on to say that faith without deeds is dead. For that reason, he can also say in verse 24 that "a person is justified by what he does and not by faith alone." The faith credited to Abraham as righteousness was a living and active faith.

4. Abraham was commanded to walk before the Lord and to be blameless. "When Abram was ninety-nine years old, the LORD appeared to him and said, 'I am God Almighty; walk before me and be blameless. I will confirm my covenant between me and you and will greatly increase your numbers'" (Gen. 17:1–2). What is significant is that walking before the Lord blamelessly is connected with confirmation of the covenant. The covenant with its promises is confirmed to Abraham, who demonstrates covenant faith and loyalty. He fulfills the obligations of the covenant.

This connection between a blameless walk and confirmation of the covenant is not artificial. This is evident from Genesis 26:3–5. Since these verses are almost never quoted in connection with Abraham, we need to pause for a moment to savor them. The Lord is speaking to Isaac after the death of Abraham. The question is what to do in the face of a famine in the land. The Lord says to Isaac,

Stay in this land for a while, and I will be with you
and will bless you. For to you and your descendants
I will give all these lands and will confirm the oath
I swore to your father Abraham. I will make your descendants as numerous as the stars in the sky and
will give them all these lands, and through your offspring all nations on earth will be blessed, *because
Abraham obeyed me and kept my requirements, my
commands, my decrees and my laws.*

Here we have a reaffirmation of the promises that are at
the heart of the Abrahamic covenant. We have the promise of
children, the land, and the presence of God himself. God con-
firms these oath-bound promises. Notice why he does this:
"Because Abraham obeyed me and kept my requirements, my
commands, my decrees and my laws." The promises are renewed and will be fulfilled *because* Abraham trusted God and
walked in righteousness according to the word of the Lord.

Also worth noting in this connection is Genesis 18:19.
The Lord is speaking about Abraham. "For I have chosen
him, so that he will direct his children and his household
after him to keep the way of the LORD by doing what is right
and just, so that the LORD will bring about for Abraham
what he has promised him." In this verse, the Lord affirms
that his electing purpose for Abraham and his children will
be fulfilled. It will be fulfilled in the way of covenant keeping. Abraham must teach his children to do what is right
and just in the eyes of the Lord *so that* the Lord will do what
he has promised to do.

**5. The history of Israel demonstrates that the promises
made to Abraham were fulfilled only as the conditions of**

the covenant were met. In Exodus 2, we read about the enslavement of Israel in Egypt. The Israelites groaned and cried out to God for relief. Verse 24 says that God remembered the covenant that he had made with Abraham, Isaac, and Jacob. It was a covenant made with Abraham and his children. Moses made the same point when the children of Israel were about to cross the Jordan: "It was because the LORD loved you and kept the oath he swore to your forefathers that he brought you out with a mighty hand and redeemed you from the land of slavery, from the power of Pharaoh king of Egypt" (Deut. 7:8). It was in fulfillment of the Abrahamic covenant that God brought Israel out of Egypt into the Promised Land.

But in fact the generation of Israelites that actually left Egypt never made it into the Promised Land. They were not permitted to enter because of their unbelief and disobedience: "And to whom did God swear that they would never enter his rest if not to those who *disobeyed?* So we see that they were not able to enter, because of their *unbelief*" (Heb. 3:18–19).

Notice both things: unbelief and disobedience. Just as faith comes to expression in obedience, so also unbelief expresses itself in disobedience. If the promises of the Abrahamic covenant had been unconditional, the Israelites would have been able to march right into the Promised Land regardless of their behavior. That did not happen. It was a new and different generation that inherited what was promised. It was a generation that believed God and moved forward at his command.

6. The ultimate proof of the conditional character of the Abrahamic covenant resides in Jesus Christ. What was it above everything else that motivated Paul in his missionary outreach to the world? It was the realization that the promises made to Abraham were being fulfilled before his very eyes. They had been realized on one level in the old covenant, when Israel entered the Promised Land. But now the promises were being fulfilled in their full scope. The nations were being discipled! The promise was that all nations on earth would be blessed through Abraham. Paul could see that beginning to happen in his own day, just as we see it continuing to happen in our day.

All of this is made possible through the covenantal righteousness of Jesus Christ. His was a living, active, and obedient faith that took him all the way to the cross. This faith was credited to him as righteousness.

Galatians 3:16 says, "The promises were spoken to Abraham and to his seed." That seed was Jesus Christ. Because Jesus was obedient unto death, even death on the cross, the promises are now being fulfilled. Galatians 3:14 says that the blessing given to Abraham comes to the Gentiles through Christ Jesus.

Nothing demonstrates the conditional character of the Abrahamic covenant more clearly than the way in which the promises of that covenant are ultimately fulfilled. They are fulfilled through the covenantal loyalty and obedience of Jesus Christ.

But just as Jesus was faithful in order to *guarantee* the blessing, so his followers must be faithful in order to *inherit* the blessing. According to the Great Commission, to be followers of Jesus we must learn to obey everything that he has commanded. We must become not only believers, but disciples! Or, to put it another way, to be a true believer is to be an obedient disciple. We must obey also by seeking to disciple others to Christ. This is the way in which the blessing promised to the nations in the Abrahamic covenant will be fulfilled!

GRACE IN THE ABRAHAMIC COVENANT

What we have seen to this point is that in the Abrahamic covenant, God's promises to Abraham and his children are in the foreground. But the Abrahamic covenant has two parts: promise and obligation. Abraham and his seed are obliged to demonstrate new obedience. They must walk with the Lord and before the Lord in the paths of faith, repentance, and obedience. In this way, the promises of the covenant are fulfilled.

For this reason, the Abrahamic covenant offers no comfort to antinomians. The promises are not unconditional. The promises will not be fulfilled irrespective of any response on the part of Abraham or his children—or, for that matter, irrespective of obedience on the part of the one seed who is Christ. The Abrahamic covenant has not one, but two parts: promise and obligation!

But does this mean that the Abrahamic covenant is really just another example of Old Testament legalism? Do the promises actually describe the reward merited by good works?

Not at all! Fulfilling the obligations of the Abrahamic covenant is never represented as meritorious achievement. The Abrahamic covenant gives no comfort to legalists, just as it gives none to antinomians. There are at least two ways to demonstrate this point.

Abraham's Use of Hagar

First, we have Abraham's attempt to receive the promise of children by sleeping with an Egyptian maidservant named

Hagar (Gen. 16). The result of that union was the birth of Ishmael. In Galatians 4, Ishmael represents the inheritance of promise by means of human effort and achievement. Hagar and Ishmael are symbols of legalism. Abraham's effort failed miserably.

Hagar and Ishmael are symbolic of human effort to achieve blessing. They are symbolic of the merit of works. This is not how the promises are realized. When God, therefore, calls for faith that is living and active, and for a blameless walk through life, he is not asking for what Abraham tried to accomplish with Hagar and Ishmael. The obedience that leads to the fulfillment of promise is totally different. It is the expression of faith and trust in the Lord, not the expression of confidence in human effort.

Entrance into the Promised Land

Second, we have the actual entrance of Israel into the Promised Land. This triumphal entry was in fulfillment of the promise to Abraham, but it happened in the way of faith and obedience. The Israelites marched in and took possession at the command of the Lord.

What is of importance here is the warning that Moses gave to the Israelites just as they were about to enter:

> After the LORD your God has driven [the Canaanites] out before you, do not say to yourself, "The LORD has brought me here to take possession of this land because of my righteousness." No, it is on account of the wickedness of these nations that the LORD is going to drive them out before you. . . . Understand, then, that it is not because of your righteousness that the LORD your God is giving you this

good land to possess, for you are a stiff-necked people. (Deut. 9:4, 6)

Moses was saying in the clearest possible way that the inheritance does not come because of human achievement or merit. Israel had not made herself worthy of receiving what was promised to Abraham. The land was a free gift of God's grace, but it could be received only by a living and active faith.

SUMMARY

The Abrahamic covenant cannot give comfort to the antinomians, but neither can it give comfort to the legalists. The Abrahamic covenant was not unconditional, but neither were its conditions meritorious. This is the light that is shed on the way of salvation by the biblical teaching on covenant.

In the Abrahamic covenant, there are promises and obligations. The blessings of the covenant are the gifts of God's free grace, and they are received by way of a living and active faith. Salvation is by grace through faith. By *grace* and through *faith!* Those are the two parts of the covenant. Now we want to see how this theme carries through into the Mosaic covenant, and from there into the new covenant.

2

The Mosaic Covenant

So far we have considered God's covenant with Abraham and his children, and we have seen that this covenant has two parts. There is both promise and obligation. In the Abrahamic covenant, promise is in the foreground, which is to say that sovereign grace is in the foreground. But the promise is not unconditional. The promise comes to fulfillment in the lives of God's people in the way of covenantal loyalty and obedience. Therefore, the Abrahamic covenant cannot give comfort to the antinomians, any more than it can give comfort to the legalists. Now we move on to consider the covenant with Moses and all Israel, and its relationship to the Abrahamic covenant.

THE COVENANT WITH MOSES AND WITH ALL ISRAEL

The great salvation event in the Old Testament is the Exodus. God brought his people out of slavery in Egypt, across the Red Sea, to Mount Sinai, where he made a covenant with them. Israel was thus established as a holy nation, the Lord's treasured possession. The Mosaic covenant was designed to regulate the life of Israel in relation to the Lord, and it would do so throughout her history, until the advent of Jesus Christ.

Whereas promise is in the foreground in the Abrahamic covenant, obligation comes to the fore in the Mosaic covenant. Several considerations demonstrate this point.

A leading feature of the Mosaic covenant is the Ten Commandments. In Exodus 34:28, these commandments are called the ten words of the covenant, and in Deuteronomy 5:3 the Ten Commandments are virtually identified with the covenant. Next to the Ten Commandments, we have the Book of the Covenant in Exodus 21–24. "Then [Moses] took the Book of the Covenant and read it to the people. They responded, 'We will do everything the LORD has said; we will obey'" (Ex. 24:7). Beyond the Book of the Covenant, we have detailed rules and regulations in the rest of Exodus, certainly in Leviticus, in Numbers, and republished in Deuteronomy. The word *obey* appears frequently in the first five books of the Bible. Again and again Israel is commanded to obey the Lord and to obey him fully. "Now if you obey me fully and keep my covenant, then out of all nations you will be my treasured possession" (Ex. 19:5).

Great blessing was promised where there is obedience to the law: "If you fully obey the LORD your God and carefully follow all his commands I give you today, the LORD your God will set you high above all the nations on earth" (Deut. 28:1). At the same time, great disaster was promised if this obedience was not forthcoming. Penalties for disobedience are found throughout the Mosaic legislation. Especially in

Deuteronomy 28 the blessings for obedience and the curses for disobedience are spelled out in great detail. The Ten Commandments are not simply ten suggestions. The law of God must be taken seriously, and it must be obeyed.

THE MOSAIC COVENANT AS A COVENANT OF WORKS

Because of the promise of blessings for obedience and the threat of punishment for disobedience, the Mosaic covenant has often been described as a *covenant of works*. It is understood to be a republication of the covenant of works that God made with Adam in the Garden of Eden, and in him with the whole human race. Representative of this view is the great Princeton theologian of a former generation, Charles Hodge.

In volume 2 of his *Systematic Theology*, Hodge says that Scripture knows only two methods of obtaining eternal life. One method demands perfect obedience and the other method demands faith. The original covenant with Adam is sometimes called a covenant of life because eternal life is promised as the reward for perfect obedience. It is frequently called a covenant of works because works are the condition on which the promise of life is suspended. Whether it is called a covenant of life or a covenant of works, the idea is the same. Life is promised on the condition of works. The new covenant, by way of contrast, promises life on the sole condition of faith. Eternal life is the gift of grace.

The basic principle embodied in this conception of the covenant of works can be called the "works/merit" principle. In the covenant of works, God is a just judge, and his creatures will be dealt with in accordance with strict principles of justice. It is a matter of simple justice to reward perfect obedience with eternal life. At the same time, the slightest infraction of the rules will forfeit eternal life.

Although the period of probation ended with Adam, the works/merit principle remains in force. If a person could present himself before God as free from sin, he would not be condemned. He would merit the reward of eternal life. However, no one will inherit eternal life in this way, because no one can present himself before the Lord as free from sin.

Although the Mosaic covenant is presented as a republication of the original covenant of works, it is generally understood to function within the context of the covenant of grace. The law serves the purposes of grace by revealing the depth of our sin and misery as we compare our lives to its perfect standard. It thereby shows the impossibility of finding eternal life by way of perfect obedience. As Paul says in Romans 7, the law reveals the sinfulness of sin. It exposes sin for the evil that it is. In this way, the law (and, more broadly, the Mosaic covenant) drives us to Christ so that we can find salvation as a free gift of grace.

Different theologians describe the covenant of works with a variety of nuances that we cannot get into here. What interests us is the idea that perfect obedience merits the reward of eternal life as a matter of simple justice. Is this how we are to understand the covenant that God made with Moses and all Israel?

THE MOSAIC COVENANT AS
A COVENANT OF GRACE

Scripture shows that the Mosaic covenant is not a covenant of works embodying a works/merit principle at its core. It is not a republication of an original covenant of works. (We must leave aside for the moment the question whether the relationship into which God entered with Adam ought to be described as a covenant of works.) Rather, the Mosaic covenant is an administration of covenant grace. At its core, the Mosaic covenant does not simply drive us to Christ, but further unfolds the gracious covenant relationship that the Lord established with Abraham and his children. The following eight considerations support the thesis that the Mosaic covenant is not a covenant of works, but an administration of covenant grace.

1. The Mosaic covenant was established in fulfillment of the covenant made with Abraham. The Israelites suffered intensely under the oppressive rule of the Egyptian pharaoh. Then they cried out to the Lord for relief, and the Lord heard their cries. "God heard their groaning and he remembered his covenant with Abraham, with Isaac and with Jacob. So God looked on the Israelites and was concerned about them" (Ex. 2:24–25). In remembrance of his covenant with Abraham, the Lord led his people out of Egypt and brought them to Mount Sinai, where he made a new covenant.

When Moses sought the favor of the Lord in the face of the sin of the golden calf, he appealed to the promises of the Abrahamic covenant: "Remember your servants Abraham, Isaac and Israel, to whom you swore by your own self: 'I will make your descendants as numerous as the stars in the sky and I will give your descendants all this land I promised them, and it will be their inheritance forever'" (Ex. 32:13). Moses appealed not on the basis of merit or achievement, but on the basis of grace.

The Lord who spoke from Mount Sinai and gave commandments to his people was the same Lord who made a covenant with Abraham and his children. The Lord promised to be Abraham's God and the God of his children (Gen. 12:1–3; 15:1–7, 18–21; 17:1–8). He renewed that covenant with Isaac (Gen. 26:2–5) and Jacob (Gen. 28:13–15). At Sinai the Israelites did not suddenly become strangers and slaves to a cold, distant, and severe judge. God, who was the friend of Abraham (2 Chron. 20:7; Isa. 41:8; James 2:23), regarded the Israelites as his children. Moses reminds them of this in Deuteronomy 14:1: "You are the children of the LORD your God." With the Mosaic covenant, the Lord did not enter into a radically different kind of relationship with his children. A relationship based on works and merit did not replace a relationship based on grace and faith.

2. The Mosaic covenant does not set aside the Abrahamic covenant. This is the point that the apostle Paul makes explicitly in Galatians 3:17. "The law, introduced 430 years later, does not set aside the covenant previously established by God and thus do away with the promise." The thought here is not simply that the Mosaic covenant comes alongside the Abrahamic covenant to function concurrently with it. The idea is not that the law reveals our sin so that we will be driven to seek grace apart from the Mosaic covenant.

Paul asks in verse 21 whether the law is "opposed to the promises of God." His answer is a resounding "Absolutely not!" But a works/merit principle would indeed be opposed to a faith/grace principle. The Mosaic covenant is not, however, opposed to the Abrahamic covenant. Nor does it run concurrently with the Abrahamic covenant while offering a totally different way of relating covenantally to the Lord. Paul is saying in Galatians 3 that the Mosaic covenant is a further unfolding of the Abrahamic covenant. The Mosaic covenant is a revelation of salvation by grace through faith.

Why was the law added to the Abrahamic covenant? It was not added to propose an alternative way of salvation that was bound to fail. Paul says it was added because of transgressions (v. 19). The law was designed to counter the devastating effect of sin in the world. The law makes clear the kind of behavior that is pleasing and honoring to the Lord and is in the best interests of humanity. It warns about the consequences of unbelief and disobedience. In the sacrificial system, it also shows Israel how to lay hold of the forgiveness graciously offered by the Lord.

Paul says in verse 24 that "the law was put in charge to lead us to Christ that we might be justified by faith." The law does not lead us away from Christ by tempting us with a way of salvation based on the merit of works. The law leads us *to* Christ. Jesus himself said, "If you believed Moses, you would believe me, for he wrote about me" (John 5:46). That is why Paul writes to Timothy that the Scriptures (inclusive of the Mosaic covenant) are able to make us "wise for salvation through faith in Christ Jesus" (2 Tim. 3:15).

3. Israel's inheritance depended on a promise. Israel was delivered from slavery in Egypt because God heard the cries of his people and remembered his covenant of promise with Abraham. It was after the deliverance that the Lord established his covenant at Mount Sinai and gave his people the Ten Commandments and other laws. These laws were obviously not given as a means whereby Israel might earn the right to be delivered from Egypt. Nor were they a means whereby Israel might earn the right to take possession of the Promised Land. In the words of Paul, "For if the inheritance depends on the law, then it no longer depends on a promise; but God in his grace gave it to Abraham through a promise" (Gal. 3:18). The inheritance of the Promised Land did not depend on law understood as a works/merit principle. The Mosaic covenant was never intended to function that way.

The Promised Land was exactly that—a *promised* land. In Deuteronomy 9:4–6, Moses reminds the Israelites that they must never say that they have taken possession of their inheritance because of their own righteousness. Rather, it is because of the Lord's righteousness in remembering his covenant that the Israelites possess the land. The Promised Land remains a promised land also after the Israelites take possession of it. It was idolatrous faithlessness and disobedience that finally brought the curse of the covenant down upon the nation. Without a living, active, penitent, and obedient faith, Israel could not remain in the Promised Land. That is the reason for the Exile toward the close of the Old Testament era. Israel's inheritance always depended on God's promise, not on meritorious achievement.

4. The Mosaic covenant is a covenant of promise. In Ephesians 2:12, Paul says that the Gentiles who have come to faith in Christ were at one time "separate from Christ . . . and foreigners to the covenants of the promise." Of special interest is the expression "covenants of the promise." It would be impossible to exclude from this expression a reference to either the Abrahamic or the Mosaic covenant.

They are placed on the same level and are called "covenants of the promise." These two covenants do not embody opposing principles of grace and works; rather, they exhibit together the principle of promise and grace.

At the heart of the covenant that God made with Abraham was the promise to be his God and the God of his children throughout the generations (Gen. 17:7). This same promise was also at the heart of the Mosaic covenant: "I will walk among you and be your God, and you will be my people" (Lev. 26:12).

The fulfillment of this promise is ultimately possible only because of the redemptive work of the Messiah. The Messiah is promised throughout the Old Testament and certainly in the Mosaic covenant. We noted earlier Jesus' word to those who challenged his identity and authority: "If you believed Moses, you would believe me, for he wrote about me" (John 5:46). We have also the word of our Lord to his disciples in Luke 24:44: "Everything must be fulfilled that is written about me in the Law of Moses, the Prophets and the Psalms." The whole sacrificial system as outlined in the Mosaic covenant is one glorious promise concerning the redemptive work of Jesus Christ.

Jesus said to those who were opposing his ministry, "You diligently study the Scriptures because you think that by them you possess eternal life. These are the Scriptures that testify about me" (John 5:39). The Scriptures, including the first five books of the Bible, promise life ultimately through faith in Jesus Christ. That is why Paul can also write that the Law and the Prophets testify to a righteousness from God apart from law conceived of as a system of merit (Rom. 3:21).

The law does not set forth a works/merit principle in

opposition to grace and faith. It testifies to the grace of God revealed in Jesus Christ. The Mosaic covenant embodies promises, and promises can be received only by faith. For Israel, the promises came wrapped in the garment of the Mosaic law. That is why faith in these promises also entailed faithfulness with respect to the commandments. Obedience is simply an expression of faith in the promises of God, not an alternative to faith.

5. The commandments were designed to separate Israel from the other nations as the Lord's treasured possession. The Lord brought his people out of Egypt as his own treasured possession. He says in Leviticus 20:24, "I am the LORD your God, who has set you apart from the nations." The laws of the Mosaic covenant were designed to preserve the distinct identity of Israel as the people of the living God. No other nation had anything like what Israel had in the Mosaic covenant. "And what other nation is so great as to have such righteous decrees and laws as this body of laws I am setting before you today?" (Deut. 4:8). "He has revealed his word to Jacob, his laws and decrees to Israel. He has done this for no other nation; they do not know his laws. Praise the LORD" (Ps. 147:19–20).

This point is especially clear in Leviticus 18:1–5. Because verse 5 is often used to show that the Mosaic covenant was a covenant of works, the passage deserves to be quoted in full:

> The LORD said to Moses, "Speak to the Israelites and say to them: 'I am the LORD your God. You must not do as they do in Egypt, where you used to live, and you must not do as they do in the land of Canaan, where I am bringing you. Do not follow their prac-

tices. You must obey my laws and be careful to follow my decrees. I am the LORD your God. Keep my decrees and laws, for the man who obeys them will live by them. I am the LORD.'"

We will come back to verse 5 later in another connection. For the moment, we want simply to note the context of that verse.

Israel's welfare depended upon her faithfulness to the Lord. Israel was not to become like the Egyptians or the Canaanites. She was to maintain her own identity and her integrity as the Lord's people by following his laws, not the customs of other nations. The law did not offer a different way of salvation to God's people. It was designed to nurture the righteousness of faith. The law served to preserve Israel in her integrity for the day when the Lord would fulfill all the promises of the covenant. Israel had to persevere in faith in order to inherit what was promised.

6. The law was designed to make Israel a holy people. When God brought his people out of Egypt, he separated them from a sinful world to be his holy people, his treasured possession. He commanded them to be holy, as he, the Lord, was holy (Lev. 11:44–45; 19:2; 20:7). The commandments showed Israel how to be the holy people that the Lord had called them to be. Various provisions of the ceremonial law were designed to remind the people of their holiness.

The laws were not given to provide a way by which Israel might earn life through her own merit. They were given to preserve Israel in the holiness in which she was established by grace when the Lord took her out of Egypt. They were given to preserve Israel in the holiness without which no one will see the Lord (Heb. 12:14).

7. *The Mosaic covenant shows that God forgives sin out of pure grace.* Broadly speaking, the laws of the Mosaic covenant may be comprehended under two headings. First, there are the laws that give direction for holy living, for personal godliness, and for righteousness in the covenant community. We often refer to these as the moral laws. They were designed to counter the pollution of sin. Second, there are the laws that show how to deal with the guilt of sin. These are the ceremonial laws that describe in great detail a system of sacrifices by means of which the Israelites experienced forgiveness.

The sacrificial system does not outline a series of chores to be done in order to gain pardon and acceptance with God. Rather, the sacrificial system reveals that our God is a gracious God. He actually wants to forgive those who sin against him, even though they do not deserve to be forgiven!

The point of the sacrificial system is not how much *we* have to do to be forgiven, but how much *God* will do. Forgiveness comes by the shedding of blood, when the penalty for sin, which is death, is paid. It comes by way of substitution: the innocent victim takes the place of the guilty sinner. In a word, the sacrificial system promises salvation through the death of Christ. Through the ceremonial laws, the benefits of Christ's atoning sacrifice were made available to believers before his advent and death on the cross.

The sacrificial system is a revelation of the grace of God, enjoyed in the way of faith. Without a living, active, and obedient faith, it is an offense against God simply to go through the motions of offering sacrifice. In Psalm 51, David acknowledges that without a penitent faith, the Lord does not delight in the burnt offerings he has commanded. "The sacrifices of God are a broken spirit; a broken and contrite heart, O God, you will not despise" (v. 17). The Lord will not be pleased with thousands of rams and ten thousand rivers of oil. He is seeking men who will act justly, love mercy, and walk humbly with their God (Mic. 6:7–8). Such men are men of faith. Without faith, sacrifices and other religious ceremonies amount to nothing. They are the "righteous acts" that are called "filthy rags" in Isaiah 64:6.

The sacrificial system is a leading feature of the Mosaic covenant. It does not exhibit a works/merit principle whereby we obtain forgiveness on the basis of something we have done. It leads us to Christ and to salvation by grace through faith in him.

8. The laws of the Mosaic covenant map out the path of life. The Lord of the Mosaic covenant is the living God and the author of life. He created human beings in his own image as living creatures. In his law, he simply teaches them how to live for their own good and for his glory.

This is the perspective from which we must view the Ten Commandments. What a privilege it would be for us, and how honoring to the Lord, if we lived in a society where there was no killing, sexual immorality, lying, or stealing. What a privilege it would be to live in a society where children honored their parents, and families kept the Lord's Day holy. Not only the Ten Commandments, but also the other rules and regulations of the Mosaic covenant, were designed to nurture and protect human life as a gift from the Creator. God intended that widows and orphans are to be cared for. Wages are to be paid in full and on time. Accused persons are not to be condemned without a hearing. These are the kinds of rules that make it possible for society to function in a decent and orderly way and to prosper.

The whole tendency of the Mosaic law is to reveal God as the living God with a passionate aversion to death and a profound love for the life he has given to his people. In Deuteronomy 32:46–47, Moses concludes his presentation of the law with these words: "Take to heart all the words I have solemnly declared to you this day, so that you may command your children to obey carefully all the words of this law. They are not just idle words for you—they are your life. By them you will live long in the land you are crossing the Jordan to possess." The law is a gracious gift that embodies wisdom for living. "Now choose life, so that you and your children may live. . . . The LORD is your life" (Deut. 30:19–20). This is also the thrust of Leviticus 18:5, "Keep my decrees and laws, for the man who obeys them will live by them. I am the LORD." This verse does not challenge Israelites to earn their salvation by their good works. Rather, it offers to all who are covenantally loyal and faithful the encouragement and assurance that they will live and prosper in the land. This is the Lord's promise to them, a promise to be received with a living and active faith.

THE TRANSFORMATION OF
THE MOSAIC COVENANT

Before we leave this point, we need to look at two passages in which Paul appears to describe the Mosaic covenant as a covenant of works. The first is Romans 10:5–6: "Moses describes in this way the righteousness that is by the law: 'The man who does these things will live by them.' But the righteousness that is by faith says: 'Do not say in your heart,

"Who will ascend into heaven?" (that is, to bring Christ down).'" The other is Galatians 3:12, "The law is not based on faith; on the contrary, 'The man who does these things will live by them.'" Both of these passages quote Leviticus 18:5, apparently as though it establishes a works/merit principle in opposition to a faith/grace principle.

In our effort to understand these passages, we need to keep several things in mind. First, Paul is writing from the perspective of the new covenant. This covenant has come in place of the Mosaic covenant. (This point will be discussed more fully in the next section.) Second, he is writing to refute the error of Jews who have rejected the claims of Christ. They insist on adherence to the Mosaic covenant to the exclusion of the new covenant. Third, Paul is also writing to refute the error of converted Jews who insist on requiring Gentiles to adhere to the provisions of the Mosaic covenant in order to become true followers of Christ. His argument is that if we insist on living under the Mosaic covenant in this way, we are alienated from Christ (Gal. 5:4). We are virtually in the same position as the Jews who have openly rejected Christ.

But, as we have seen, the Mosaic covenant is a revelation of the Christ to come. A Mosaic covenant without Christ is not the covenant that the Lord established with his people at Mount Sinai. Without Christ, the Mosaic covenant is transformed into a covenant of works. People who seek to live under this transformed covenant are seeking to establish their own righteousness (Phil. 3:9). They are seeking to achieve salvation by their own human effort (Gal. 3:3).

In the course of his refutation, Paul uses an *ad hominem* argument by quoting Scripture according to the sense in which his opponents understand it. Those who seek righteousness by means of the Mosaic covenant as a works/merit principle have not met the standard they set for themselves. "The man who does these things will live by them"—but they have not done these things. Paul writes at the end of his letter to the Galatians, "Not even those who are circumcised obey the law, yet they want you to be circumcised that they may boast about your flesh" (6:13). In Romans 2, Paul condemns those who call themselves Jews and rely on the law, because they flagrantly transgress the law. Because of this, God's name has been blasphemed among the Gentiles.

When the law is conceived of as a works/merit scheme, Paul is opposed to the law. But he makes clear in Galatians 3:15–18 that the law as the Lord gave it was never intended to function in that way. The Mosaic covenant does not set aside the Abrahamic covenant.

The law leads to Christ, not away from Christ. In order now to be faithful to Moses and to uphold the law, one must submit to Christ in faith and say farewell to life under the Mosaic system. Paul's opponents claimed to be faithful to the Mosaic covenant, but they rejected the Christ of whom Moses spoke. Without Christ, the sacrificial system is pointless and the commandments are powerless. A revelation of grace is thereby transformed into a system of meritorious achievement.

SUMMARY

In the Mosaic covenant, the Lord did not establish a covenant of works with his people. He did not establish a covenant on the basis of a principle that is the very opposite of that on which the Abrahamic covenant is founded.

The Mosaic covenant is not a covenant of works, but a "covenant of love." This is the happy translation found in the New International Version at Deuteronomy 7:9: "Know therefore that the LORD your God is God; he is the faithful God, keeping his *covenant of love* to a thousand generations of those who love him and keep his commands." The phrase is also found at several other places in the Old Testament (Deut. 7:12; 1 Kings 8:23; 2 Chron. 6:14; Neh. 1:5; 9:32; Dan. 9:4).

God does not tempt his children to try to earn their salvation by the merit of their works. Nor does he tease them by offering a way of salvation that he knows will not work. More pointedly, the very idea of merit is foreign to the way in which God our Father relates to his children. Rather, in love the Lord leads his people to trust him. In the Mosaic covenant, he teaches his people how to live happy and productive lives in the Promised Land in union and communion with the Lord of the covenant. He promises forgiveness of sins and eternal life, not as something to be earned, but as a gift to be received by a living and active faith.

Like the Abrahamic covenant, the Mosaic covenant has two parts, promise and obligation. In the Abrahamic covenant, the focus is on promise. In the Mosaic covenant, the focus is on obligation—but promise does not recede into the background. The Mosaic covenant is a revelation of the Christ who is to come.

The obedience required of Israel is not the obedience of merit, but the obedience of faith. It is the fullness of faith. Obedience is simply faithfulness to the Lord; it is the righteousness of faith (compare Rom. 9:32). This point comes out with special clarity in Hebrews 11, where we see what the patriarchs accomplished by faith. "By faith Abraham, when called to go to a place he would later receive as his inheritance, obeyed and went, even though he did not know where he was going" (v. 8). "By faith Abraham, when God tested him, offered Isaac as a sacrifice" (v. 17). Later in the chapter, we see that those who lived under the Mosaic covenant were obedient to the Lord and through faith "gained what was promised" (v. 33).

In all of this, we can see that the Abrahamic and Mosaic covenants do not exhibit opposing principles of grace and merit, or of faith and works. In both covenants there are promises, and these promises are received by a living and active faith. In both covenants, there are warnings about the consequences of unbelief and disobedience. The Lord says to Abraham in Genesis 17:14, "Any uncircumcised male, who has not been circumcised in the flesh, will be cut off from his people; he has broken my covenant." The penalties threatened for disobedience in the Mosaic covenant are fully in line with this provision of the Abrahamic covenant.

Threatened curses for disobedience do not transform either the Abrahamic covenant or the Mosaic covenant into a covenant of works. The law is not a self-help scheme, but light in the darkness. It is wisdom along the way. The law does indeed condemn sin, and it pronounces judgment on ungodliness. But Isaiah describes God's work of judgment as his "strange work"; it is his "alien task" (Isa. 28:21). The law was designed to nurture and encourage God-honoring holiness. Those who walk in the ways of the Lord will never be put to shame. This is the word of promise and encouragement that the Lord makes in Psalm 103:17–18: "But from everlasting to everlasting the LORD's love is with those who fear him, and his righteousness with their children's children—with those who keep his covenant and remember to obey his precepts."

Obedience in the Mosaic covenant is not meritorious achievement, but the expression of faith. For this reason, legalists can derive no support from the Mosaic covenant, just as antinomians can derive no comfort from the Abrahamic covenant.

Now the question becomes, how does all of this relate to the new covenant? As children of the new covenant, can we continue to sing Psalm 103? That will be our concern in the next chapter.

ॐ 3

The New Covenant

We have seen that the Abrahamic and Mosaic covenants have two parts, promise and obligation. In the Abrahamic covenant, promise is in the foreground. In the Mosaic covenant, obligation comes to the fore, but promise does not recede into the background. Rather, the promise of salvation through the Messiah is enriched. Now we come to the new covenant. How does it relate to what has gone before?

JESUS ESTABLISHES A NEW COVENANT

With the advent of Jesus, a new covenant is established. In Jeremiah 31:31, the Lord says, "The time is coming when I will make a new covenant with the house of Israel and with the house of Judah." Hebrews 8:7–13 shows that this promise is fulfilled in the ministry of Jesus Christ. Jesus calls it a new covenant when he institutes the sacrament of the Lord's Supper: "This cup is the new covenant in my blood, which is poured out for you" (Luke 22:20). Jesus is the mediator of a new covenant (Heb. 9:15; 12:24). Paul

COVENANT LIGHT ON THE WAY OF SALVATION

says that God has made us ministers of a new covenant (2 Cor. 3:6).

We discover in the New Testament that the new covenant, like the Abrahamic and Mosaic covenants, also has two parts, promise and obligation. We will look at each of these parts separately. Then we will consider how they are related to each other and how this new covenant relates to the Abrahamic and Mosaic covenants that preceded it.

The Promises of the New Covenant

We begin with the promise side of the new covenant. The new covenant came in fulfillment of promises made under the old covenant, but Hebrews 8:6 says that the new covenant is founded upon better promises than the old. Hebrews 9:15 indicates what those better promises are: "Christ is the mediator of a new covenant, that those who are called may receive the promised eternal inheritance—now that he has died as a ransom to set them free from the sins committed under the first covenant." The promised eternal inheritance comes through the mediation of Jesus Christ. This promise of eternal life is certainly in the foreground in the new covenant. Jesus says, "I have come that they may have life, and have it to the full" (John 10:10). First John 2:25 says, "This is what he promised us—even eternal life." God promises the crown of life to those who love him (James 1:12). On the Day of Judgment, those who belong to Jesus by faith will enter into eternal life. "Believe in the Lord Jesus, and you will be saved" (Acts 16:31). Jesus appeared once on earth to take away sin. "He will appear a second time, not to bear sin, but to bring salvation to those who are waiting for him" (Heb. 9:28). Those who persevere in faith will receive what Jesus has promised (Heb. 10:36).

The gospel promises pardon for sin and acceptance by God. It promises eternal life after the final judgment. "Therefore, there is now no condemnation for those who are in Christ Jesus" (Rom. 8:1). "We have peace with God through our Lord Jesus Christ" (Rom. 5:1). It is no wonder that 2 Peter 1:4 speaks of the "very great and precious promises" that are ours in the new covenant.

We need only be reminded that the promises of the new covenant point to sovereign, undeserved grace. As Romans 4:16 says with respect to the Abrahamic covenant, "The promise comes by faith, so that it may be by grace and may be guaranteed to all Abraham's offspring." The new covenant, which takes up, unfolds, and fulfills the ancient promises, exhibits the same principle. The benefits of the new covenant are received by grace through faith. "By grace you have been saved, through faith . . . not by works, so that no one can boast" (Eph. 2:8–9).

The Obligations of the New Covenant

Promise is one part of the new covenant, and obligation is the other part. In the new covenant, obligation is no less prominent than promise. However, because it frequently receives less attention than the promises, this side of the new covenant deserves to be treated at greater length.

First, those who are in covenant with the Lord and who have received the promise of eternal life are obliged to believe. The promises of the new covenant are received and made fruitful by *faith*.

Reference has already been made to Ephesians 2:8–9 ("By grace you have been saved, through faith . . . not by works, so that no one can boast") and to Acts 16:31 ("Believe in the Lord Jesus, and you will be saved"). As Jesus fulfilled his earthly ministry, he called upon the ancient covenant people to believe in him as their promised Messiah. The gospel is summarized in John 3:16: "For God so loved the world that he gave his one and only Son, that whoever believes in him shall not perish but have eternal life." Paul declares, "I am not ashamed of the gospel, because it is the power of God for the salvation of everyone who believes: first for the Jew, then for the Gentile" (Rom. 1:16). The gospel demands faith because, as Paul says, "the promise comes by faith" (Rom. 4:16). The gospel declares that Jesus Christ alone is Lord and Savior. Salvation can be found nowhere else than in him. Therefore, the gospel invites and commands all people everywhere to entrust themselves to Jesus, to receive, accept, and rest upon him as Lord and Savior.

Second, right along with faith, the new covenant calls for *repentance*. John the Baptist prepared the way for our Lord and for the new covenant by demanding repentance: "Repent, for the kingdom of heaven is near" (Matt. 3:2). Jesus similarly demanded repentance when he began his ministry: "From that time on Jesus began to preach, 'Repent, for the kingdom of heaven is near'" (Matt. 4:17). The disciples followed the example set by their Lord. Mark 6:12 says, "They went out and preached that people should repent."

Peter's message on the Day of Pentecost concluded with a ringing call to repentance (Acts 2:38). Paul's message to the Greeks in Athens sounded the same note: God "commands all people everywhere to repent" (Acts 17:30). When Paul gives an accounting of his ministry, he says, "I have declared to both Jews and Greeks that they must turn to God in repentance and have faith in our Lord Jesus" (Acts 20:21). Notice how Paul calls his hearers not simply to faith, but to faith and repentance. In the last book of the Bible, the letters to the seven churches of Asia Minor all demand repentance (Rev. 2–3).

The New Testament, as well as the Old, clearly teaches that repentance entails more that just sorrow for sin. Repentance includes turning away from sin and making a new beginning. When Paul defends his ministry before King Agrippa, he says, "First to those in Damascus, then to those in Jerusalem and in all Judea, and to the Gentiles also, I preached that they should repent and turn to God and prove their repentance by their deeds" (Acts 26:20). Faith and repentance are indissolubly intertwined with one another. You cannot turn to Christ in faith without turning away from what is opposed to Christ in repentance.

Third, faith produces repentance, and repentance is evident in the lifestyle of the believer. Thus, the obligations of the new covenant include not only faith and repentance, but also *obedience*.

It is striking that the public ministry of Jesus began with the Sermon on the Mount. Various writers have pointed out the similarity between the beginning of the Mosaic covenant and the beginning of the new covenant. As the Lord God came to Mount Sinai to deliver his commandments to Moses and all Israel, so also the Lord Jesus came to another mount to deliver the commandments of the new covenant to his disciples and to the church of the new covenant. The Sermon on the Mount is a detailed revelation of the righteousness of the kingdom of God. Jesus makes clear that he did not come to abolish the Law or the Prophets. Far from abolishing covenant obligation, Jesus says, "Unless your righteousness surpasses that of the Pharisees and the teachers of the law, you will certainly not enter the kingdom of heaven" (Matt. 5:20).

Jesus concluded his public ministry with what we call the Great Commission. In giving this missionary mandate, Jesus told his followers to make disciples of the nations. Disciples not only believe with their minds, but also obey with their hands and feet. Jesus says that his disciples must be taught "to obey everything I have commanded you" (Matt. 28:19–20). "You are my friends if you do what I command" (John 15:14). "If you obey my commands, you will remain in my love, just as I have obeyed my Father's commands and remain in his love" (John 15:10).

In becoming incarnate for our salvation, Jesus humbled himself. Paul says that Jesus became obedient to death— even death on a cross (Phil. 2:8). Those who claim to live in him and to have life in him "must walk as Jesus did" (1 John 2:6). They must become obedient, as he was obedient. "The man who says, 'I know him,' but does not do what he commands is a liar, and the truth is not in him" (1 John 2:4). "And this is his command: to believe in the name of his Son, Jesus Christ, and to love one another as he commanded us" (1 John 3:23). This last verse is most striking. Even faith itself is a matter of obedience to the command of our Lord.

Fourth, beyond the calls to faith, repentance, and obedience, we have the call to *perseverance*. The book of Hebrews is quite significant in this respect. The whole book is a call to those who have professed faith in Jesus to persevere in that faith. "We must pay more careful attention, therefore, to what we have heard, so that we do not drift away. . . . How shall we escape if we ignore such a great salvation?" (Heb. 2:1, 3). Similarly, Hebrews 10:35–36 exhorts the readers, "So do not throw away your confidence; it will be richly rewarded. You need to persevere so that when you have done the will of God, you will receive what he has promised."

Notice that it is not simply perseverance in *belief*, but perseverance in *doing the will of God*. This is the way in which you receive what has been promised as a gift of sovereign grace. Hebrews 10:35–36 comes at the very end of the chapter. Hebrews 11 goes on to cite example after example of persons living under the Abrahamic and Mosaic covenants who so persevered. They believed and acted accordingly. In this way, they received what was promised. Hebrews 11 presents these persons as examples for us who live under the new covenant, because the same principles are operative in all the covenants.

Fifth, the obedience called for in the new covenant is a necessary response to the gospel, not simply because the Lord demands it, but also because of the consequences of unbelief, impenitence, disobedience, and a failure to persevere (backsliding). The consequence of unbelief is condemnation: "Whoever believes in him is not condemned, but whoever does not believe stands condemned already because he has not believed in the name of God's one and only Son" (John 3:18). The consequence of impenitence is death: "Unless you repent, you too will all perish" (Luke 13:3, 5). The consequence of disobedience is exclusion from the kingdom of heaven: "Not everyone who says to me, 'Lord, Lord,' will enter the kingdom of heaven, but only he who does the will of my Father who is in heaven" (Matt. 7:21). The consequence of backsliding is destruction: "If anyone does not remain in me, he is like a branch that is thrown away and withers; such branches are picked up, thrown into the fire and burned" (John 15:6).

These warnings come from the ministry of the Lord

himself, and the apostles echo them. Paul writes in Galatians 6:7–8, "Do not be deceived: God cannot be mocked. A
man reaps what he sows. The one who sows to please his
sinful nature, from that nature will reap destruction; the one
who sows to please the Spirit, from the Spirit will reap eternal life."

We have seen that the new covenant has these two
parts, promise and obligation. But how do these two parts
relate to each other?

The Relationship Between Promise and Obligation

Promise and obligation in the new covenant are related
in the same way that they are related in the Abrahamic and
Mosaic covenants. As we have already seen, the benefits
and blessings of the new covenant are pure grace. Eternal
life is promised as an undeserved gift from the Lord. He forgives our sins and receives us as righteous because of Jesus
Christ and his redemptive accomplishment on our behalf.
At the same time, faith, repentance, obedience, and perseverance are indispensable to the enjoyment of these blessings. They are conditions, but they are not meritorious
conditions. Faith is required, but faith looks away from personal merit to the promises of God. Repentance and obedience flow from faith as the fullness of faith. This is
faithfulness, and faithfulness is perseverance in faith. A living, active, and abiding faith is the way in which the believer enters into eternal life.

James asks rhetorically, "What good is it, my brothers,
if a man claims to have faith but has no deeds? Can such
faith save him?" (James 2:14). The implied answer is "No,
of course not!" Even here in James 2, eternal life is a free
gift, unearned and unmerited, but it must be received by

a penitent and obedient faith. Repentance and obedience are necessary, but they are not the meritorious grounds of our acceptance with God. Salvation remains a gift of God's free grace.

The relationship between promise and obligation in the new covenant can be illustrated by reference to 1 Corinthians 10:1–13. In this passage, Paul draws upon the experience of Israel to give a warning to the Corinthian church. In verses 1–4, Paul establishes the validity of the comparison. Our forefathers enjoyed the same covenant blessing and privilege that we now do. However, they rebelled against the Lord and were disobedient. The Lord punished them with death in the wilderness, so that they could not enter the Promised Land. This serves as a warning to us not to follow their example, lest we also perish as they did. "So, if you think you are standing firm, be careful that you don't fall!" (v. 12).

Note that Paul can take an example from life under the Mosaic covenant and apply it to those who live under the new covenant. This shows that the principles operative under both covenants are the same. There is promise and there is obligation. The land promised to the wilderness generation was the Promised Land. It was an unearned and unmerited gift of grace. Yet the first generation did not inherit the land because of their unbelief and disobedience. This is the point made in Hebrews 3:18–19. Similarly for us, eternal life is an undeserved gift of grace; we enter into it by way of a living, active, and obedient faith.

The relationship between promise and obligation is also illustrated in Hebrews 10:35–36: "So do not throw away your confidence; it will be richly rewarded. You need to persevere so that when you have done the will of God, you will receive what he has promised." The requirement is perseverance in faith, which includes doing the will of God. The benefit is receiving what God has promised. But what is promised cannot be earned or merited. It is received as a gift of pure grace.

The new covenant is new, but it maintains continuity with what precedes it. It is not new in the sense that it introduces a principle of faith/grace as opposed to a principle of works/merit. Psalm 25:10 remains valid under the new covenant as well as under the Mosaic: "All the ways of the LORD are loving and faithful for those who keep the demands of his covenant." We can continue to sing Psalm 103 and the rest of the Psalms as well.

THE ABROGATION OF
THE MOSAIC COVENANT

At this point, the question naturally arises, Why was the Mosaic covenant set aside? If the new covenant shows the same pattern of promise and obligation as the Mosaic, why was the Mosaic covenant abrogated? Why is the new covenant not simply added to the Mosaic covenant, as the Mosaic covenant was added to the Abrahamic covenant?

It is not necessary to review in detail the evidence for the abrogation of the Mosaic covenant. Some of that evidence will appear in the course of the discussion that follows. The Jerusalem council settled this issue (Acts 15). Gentile converts to Christ do not need to be circumcised or to obey the law of Moses. The new covenant is established in place of the Mosaic covenant. But why? Why was the Mosaic covenant abrogated?

The Mosaic covenant is a yoke of slavery. This question is often answered by saying that the Mosaic covenant was a covenant of works that taught salvation by human effort. The new covenant teaches salvation by grace and has taken the place of the old covenant. In writing to the Galatians, Paul calls the law of Moses nothing less than "a yoke of slavery" (5:1). In his address to the Jerusalem council, Peter calls the law of Moses "a yoke that neither we nor our fathers have been able to bear" (Acts 15:10). It is tempting to find the reason for this negative characterization of the law residing in a works/merit principle. The law of Moses was a yoke of slavery because it required us to earn or merit our own salvation, and we were totally unable to do that because of our sin. The temptation ought to be resisted, however, because there are other reasons why the law could be described as a yoke of slavery.

First, the law of Moses required an elaborate and complex ritual for temple worship. Both the quantity and the quality of animal and other sacrifices imposed quite a burden on the community. Beyond that, later interpreters of the law imposed all sorts of additional rules and regulations. Jesus said that the teachers of the law and the Pharisees who sat in Moses seat "tie up heavy loads and put them on men's shoulders" (Matt. 23:4).

Second and more profoundly, sinful human nature reacts negatively to the righteousness required in the law. The law is good, but in the sinner it provokes a spirit of hostility and rebellion, bringing him under the curse of the law rather than receiving its blessing (Rom. 7:8). In this way, the law became a yoke of slavery rather than the charter of liberty that David and James found it to be. James calls it "the perfect law that gives freedom" (James 1:25). David says, "I will walk about in freedom, for I have sought out your precepts" (Ps. 119:45).

The third and most significant reason why the law is a yoke of slavery will become clear as we proceed.

The Mosaic covenant is defective and obsolete. The Mosaic covenant was not set aside because it embodied a works/merit principle. The New Testament tells us quite explicitly why it was set aside. The Mosaic covenant was abrogated because it was defective and had become obsolete.

Hebrews 8:7 says, "For if there had been nothing wrong with that first covenant, no place would have been sought for another." There was something wrong with the Mosaic covenant. It was defective because it could not succeed in doing what it was designed to do. The Mosaic covenant was designed to deal with the problem of sin by providing a way of salvation. Specifically, it was designed to do two things. The *sacrificial system* was designed to take away both the penalty of sin and sin itself. The *commandments* were designed to teach the Israelites how to live acceptably before God as his covenant partners.

The defect in the law was correspondingly twofold. First, the blood of bulls and goats could not really handle the problem of sin. Hebrews 10:4 says that "it is impossible for the blood of bulls and goats to take away sins." Second, the commandments could not impart life. Galatians 3:21 says, "If a law had been given that could impart life, then righteousness would certainly have come by the law." The commandments could teach a person how to live, but they could not impart life to a sinner dead in his trespasses and sins. For both of these reasons, Israel never succeeded in being the holy people of God that the Lord called them to be under the Mosaic covenant. That covenant was faulty. It was defective. That is why it was set aside when Jesus established the new covenant.

When we say that the Mosaic covenant in itself could not really deal with the problem of sin or impart life, we are not saying that no one who lived under this covenant up to the time of Christ could be saved. They could be saved, but ultimately only because of the Christ to come. The Mosaic system was valid and efficacious as the God-given way of salvation prior to the advent of Jesus because it was the means by which believing and covenantally loyal Israelites had access to the benefits of salvation to be secured by Christ in the fullness of time.

The advent of Christ himself made this Mosaic covenant obsolete. First, the blood of bulls and goats cannot take away sin, but the blood of Jesus can and does take away sin. Second, the commandments cannot impart life, but the resurrection of Jesus from the dead can and does impart life. The new covenant makes the old and defective covenant obsolete. "By calling this covenant 'new,' he has made the first one obsolete; and what is obsolete and aging will soon disappear" (Heb. 8:13). The death and resurrection of Jesus accomplished what the Mosaic system could never in itself accomplish. "Through [Jesus] everyone who believes is justified from everything you could not be justified from by the law of Moses" (Acts 13:39).

If the Mosaic covenant is obsolete and has been set aside, to cling to it after the death and resurrection of Christ is really to alienate yourself from Christ. This is what Paul says in Galatians 5:4: "You who are trying to be justified by law have been alienated from Christ; you have fallen away from grace." In isolation from Christ, the Mosaic covenant is transformed into a works/merit scheme whereby a person seeks to achieve his own salvation by what he does. As we have seen, this is what the Pharisees and others did to the law in the days of our Lord. They used the Mosaic covenant in a way that it was never intended to function.

There is also this significant point to be noted. The Mosaic covenant, as promulgated on Mount Sinai, was filled with the promise of the Christ to come. Through its provisions, a believer under that covenant laid hold of the benefits that could come only through Christ. But, as a matter of historical fact, Jesus had not yet come! His advent in Bethlehem was yet in the future. Therefore, from a historical perspective, the Mosaic covenant did function in isolation from Christ. For that reason, Israel failed miserably to be the people the Lord had called them to be. In this sense, they were indeed under a yoke of slavery. This is the third and most significant reason why the law is a yoke of slavery, as indicated above.

Paul says in Romans 8:3–4 that the law was powerless because it was weakened by sinful human nature. But what the law could not do, God has done in the fullness of time by sending his Son. His Son deals definitively with the problem of sin, with both the guilt and the pollution of sin, "in order that the righteous requirements of the law might be fully met in us, who do not live according to the sinful nature but according to the Spirit."

Paul declares repeatedly that observing the law cannot save a person. The reason for this is not that no one can keep the law perfectly as a covenant of works. Rather, observing the law cannot save a person because the Mosaic system is no longer operative. Salvation comes through faith in Jesus Christ. The Mosaic covenant has been abrogated because it was defective and obsolete. It has been set aside.

Similarly, when Paul says that we are not under law, but under grace (Rom. 6:14–15), he does not mean that we are free from any obligation to keep the commandments. Rather, we are free from the law in the sense that we do not serve the Lord by fulfilling the provisions of the Mosaic covenant, as though that covenant arrangement were still operative. The Mosaic covenant has been abrogated. But such freedom is obviously not a license for immorality. "You, my brothers, were called to be free. But do not use your freedom to indulge the sinful nature; rather, serve one another in love" (Gal. 5:13).

By way of summary, the new covenant and the Mosaic covenant are not opposed to each other as two different ways of salvation, one offering salvation by faith and the other by works. The Lord God never taught his people to save themselves by their good works on the basis of merit. The Abrahamic, Mosaic, and new covenants are all revelations of salvation by grace through faith. Like the Abrahamic and Mosaic covenants, the new covenant has two parts: promise and obligation. What is new is not the principle of grace, but the person and work of Jesus Christ. In him all the promises are "yes" and "amen" (2 Cor. 1:20). In Jesus we are enabled to become the covenant keepers that God intended us to be from the beginning.

The structure of the new covenant can give no comfort to the legalists because salvation is a matter of gracious promise, not meritorious achievement. But at the same time, the new covenant gives no comfort to the antinomians. The free gift of salvation is received through faith, and saving faith is not a dead faith, but a living and active faith.

ఈ4

Conclusion

The time has now come for us to return to the subject with which we began. Is there any hope for a common understanding between Roman Catholicism and evangelical Protestantism regarding the way of salvation? May I suggest that there is at least a glimmer of hope if both sides are willing to embrace a covenantal understanding of the way of salvation.

ROMAN CATHOLICISM

According to traditional Roman Catholic doctrine, salvation is by grace through faith. Romanism means by this that the church offers help, and this help is grace. The help of the church is received by faith. At the same time, the official pronouncements of the Council of Trent in the sixteenth century, made in response to the Protestant Reformation, make clear that salvation is a reward for good works. With help from the church and its sacramental system, a sinner becomes a righteous person. By his good works, this righteous person merits the reward eternal life because of what he is and what he does.

In support of its view, Rome appeals not simply to its doctrinal tradition, but also to the Bible. Rome certainly appeals to James 2:24: "You see that a person is justified by what he does and not by faith alone." Rome also appeals to Paul in Galatians 5:6: "For in Christ Jesus neither circumcision nor uncircumcision has any value. The only thing that counts is faith expressing itself through love." And Romans 2:7 says, "To those who by persistence in doing good seek glory, honor and immortality, [God] will give eternal life." There are many other passages of similar import to be found in the Bible. Rome claims that such passages of Scripture are not allowed to function positively or constructively in the Protestant doctrine of salvation. Rather, they are put to one side and are dealt with as problems to be solved.

Roman Catholic teaching is faulty on two related but distinct levels. On one level, Rome's doctrine of salvation requires that place be given to human merit. This is clear from the decrees of the Council of Trent. But if there is place for human merit, then there is place for boasting about meritorious achievement. However, Paul says in Ephesians 2:8–9, "For it is by grace you have been saved, through faith—and this not from yourselves, it is the gift of God—not by works, so that no one can boast." Our boast must be in the work of God, not in our own works. "For we are God's workmanship, created in Christ Jesus to do good works, which God prepared in advance for us to do" (v. 10).

But on a deeper level, what must be challenged in the Roman Catholic doctrine is the very idea of merit itself. God does not, and never did, relate to his people on the basis of a works/merit principle. The biblical texts to which Rome appeals must be read in the light of the covenant. Then the biblical demands for repentance and obedience, together with the warnings against disobedience, can be seen for what they are. They are not an invitation to achieve salvation by human merit. They are a call to find salvation wholly and exclusively in Jesus Christ through faith in him. It is the biblical doctrine of covenant that challenges Roman Catholicism at its root.

What is required from Rome is a change from a works/merit paradigm for understanding the way of salvation to a covenantal paradigm. Such a change would, of course, require repudiation of some key declarations of the Council of Trent. Whether that is possible is a subject for another occasion. At the same time, this change in paradigm would provide a proper basis for Rome's legitimate insistence that full credence be given to James 2:24, Galatians 5:6, and similar passages. In light of the covenant, these texts do function in our understanding of the way of salvation without a lapse into the error of legalism.

EVANGELICAL PROTESTANTISM

For its part, evangelical Protestantism has always insisted that salvation is wholly by God's grace. We have rightly rejected the idea that a human being can do anything to achieve his own salvation. We have rightly rejected the idea that a person can work to merit the reward of eternal life. However, we have not always rejected the very idea of merit itself. The consequence is twofold.

First, if we do not reject the idea of merit, we are not really able to challenge the Romanist doctrine of salvation at its very root. Either we have to grant that the good works of the believer are indeed meritorious, allowing us to boast in our own personal achievement, or we have to deny that the good works of the believer are really good. In that case, we are saying that sanctification amounts to nothing. If we do not challenge the idea that good works are meritorious, the necessity for sanctification and the fact that believers do perform good works always represent a threat to salvation by grace.

The second consequence of not rejecting the idea of merit is that we feel threatened by passages of Scripture that speak of repentance and obedience as conditions for entering eternal life. Passages like Galatians 5:6 and James 2:24, to which Rome appeals, are almost uniformly treated as problem texts because they do not fit into a noncovenantal paradigm of salvation by grace. Various exegetical and dogmatic devices of dubious validity are used to defuse and tame these texts so that they do fit.

We want to ward off the clear danger of legalism, but in doing so, we gravitate toward antinomianism. Then, in order to ward off antinomianism, we are compelled to introduce a measure of legalism. After all, good works, if they are truly good, are meritorious. This is the dilemma that has plagued evangelicalism even to our day, as evidenced by the lordship salvation controversy and the more recent discussion surrounding *The Gift of Salvation* and the *Appeal to Fellow Evangelicals*.

In terms of the questions posed at the beginning, the issue is this: How do you preach grace without suggesting that it makes no difference what your lifestyle is like? And how do you preach repentance without calling into question salvation by grace apart from works?

COVENANT PERSPECTIVE

The answer to this dilemma is to be found in the doctrine of the covenant, with its two parts, promise and obligation. In keeping with his eternal purpose, the Lord God brings us into covenant with himself. All of the blessings of the covenant are ours as gifts of sovereign grace. The covenantal demand for faith, repentance, and obedience is simply the way in which the Lord leads us into possession of these blessings.

Salvation is both by *grace* and through *faith*. These are the two parts of the covenant: grace and faith, promise and obligation. Grace is not without conditions, and a living and active faith is not meritorious achievement. It is the biblical doctrine of covenant that enables us to sail safely between the Scylla of legalism and the Charybdis of antinomianism.

As we look back at the documents mentioned earlier (*Evangelicals and Catholics Together; The Gift of Salvation; An Appeal to Fellow Evangelicals; The Gospel of Jesus Christ: An Evangelical Celebration*), what is striking is the total absence of any appeal to the covenant. This is striking, but not surprising. The covenant plays almost no role, either in the Roman Catholic doctrine of salvation, or in the thinking of many evangelical Christians. Progress can be made in the discussion among evangelicals by letting the light of the covenant shine on the way of salvation. In this same light, there might even be the hope of progress in the ongoing controversy between Rome and the Reformation.

We need to learn to think covenantally. To think covenantally is to think biblically. To think biblically is simply to be loyal to our Savior, Jesus Christ, the Lord of the covenant.

PART 2

Covenant Light on Evangelism

Reformed pastors continue to wrestle with the need to develop an evangelistic methodology that is consistent with the Calvinistic theology they believe and teach. Those who are opposed to Reformed theology frequently maintain that zeal for evangelism cannot coexist with zeal for the Reformed faith. They argue that a pastor can be either a good evangelist or a good Calvinist, but not both at the same time. When we survey the modern religious landscape, it often seems as though churches with an evangelistic methodology that can be characterized as more or less Arminian are large and fast growing. Churches that are resolutely Calvinistic are often small and not very impressive. It almost seems as though the purer the doctrine, the fewer the people.

Of course, we can dispute the accuracy and the significance of the statistics by saying, for example, that the numbers are inflated and that many of those who have made a decision for Christ are not really converted. But no Calvinist should take comfort from the thought that on the Judgment Day the Arminians may turn out to have been less effective as evangelists than they appeared to be. Even if this were to prove true, it would not glorify God, and the shortcomings of Arminian-style evangelism would not automatically commend methods used by Reformed pastors.

We can find various reasons why zeal for evangelism and zeal for the Reformed faith don't appear to go together.

Some would argue that the main problem is the particularism of the Reformed faith. By particularism, we mean the doctrine of election and all that flows from it. God has chosen those whom he will save. He sent his Son to die on the cross for them only and sends his Holy Spirit to convert only those who are elect. Those who are not elected for salvation are reprobate and will not be saved. The doctrines of election and reprobation would appear to make it inherently impossible to present the gospel as good news to modern man. The gospel would hardly appear to be good news to the reprobate, and since no one knows for sure who the elect are, no word of encouragement, comfort, or assurance can be addressed directly to them as such. As a result, we tend to proclaim the gospel in the third person, talking in terms of what Christ has done for "his own." But the question remains: What good news can a pastor give to this or that particular person? What good news does the gospel have for me?

A related problem has to do with the place of the law and the response of obedience in evangelism. Consistently Reformed pastors want nothing to do with "easy believism." This is a way of presenting the gospel that separates acceptance of Christ as Savior from acceptance of him as Lord. The Bible teaches that without sanctification, or holiness of life, no one will see the Lord (Heb. 12:14). Therefore, it is not enough to ask the sinner for a simple act of faith. The evangelist must also demand repentance. But the difficulty here is that the opposite of "easy believism" often turns out to be "hard work–ism," and that is not very good news. Indeed, in terms of Paul's argument in Romans and Galatians, that destroys the gospel.

In any case, how can we demand faith or repentance or

obedience when the basic response is not determined by the free will of the sinner, but by the sovereign choice of God, who elects whom he wills? Beyond that, how can we attain the assurance of being in a state of grace and salvation without a direct knowledge of our eternal election? We are told that the results of election and regeneration can be seen in the changed lifestyle of the believer, but then we are also reminded of the danger of misunderstanding and self-deception. We are told that as Christians we are still sinners, and that there is only a small beginning of new obedience in even the best of us. Honest and searching self-examination would appear to yield more reason for doubt than for assurance.

These questions are not new, and they have not remained unanswered in the history of Reformed theology. For example, those who followed the lead provided by Karl Barth responded to the challenge by saying that all persons are in Christ, and that in him they are simultaneously elect and reprobate. They are confident that the "yes" of God will prevail over his "no." This answer is of course unacceptable to anyone committed to the historic Reformed faith as the authentic expression of biblical Christianity.

Others have come to terms with these problems by saying simply that here we have to do with a paradox that cannot be explained. They are content to teach like Calvinists and preach like Arminians. They are content to have an intellectual commitment to the five points of Calvinism and a practical commitment to the five points of the Remonstrance. (The Canons of Dordt [1619], which set forth the five points of Calvinism, were written as a response to the Arminian Remonstrance [1610].) Still others, not content with a compromise, have sought to show how the particularism of Calvinism does not conflict with the free offer of the gospel, how law is consistent with grace, and how the priority of regeneration (the new birth) to faith does not impinge upon the demand for faith. This labor has not been entirely unfruitful. Nevertheless, the persistence of the questions may not be ascribed entirely to human perversity. It may well be indicative of the fact that we have not used all of the resources of the Reformed faith to find satisfactory answers.

The five points formulated by the Synod of Dordt are biblical, and they are essential to full-orbed Calvinism, but they do not exhaust Calvinism. Just as biblical and just as essential is the doctrine of the covenant. In what follows, I am proposing that what the Bible says about covenant affords the perspective from which we ought to approach our evangelistic task, not only with respect to the baptized youth of the church, but also with respect to our mission in the world. From this perspective, it becomes clear that the gospel is good news without reservation and without embarrassment, and that as good news the gospel is the power of God for salvation for all who believe.

We begin by seeking to understand the Great Commission from the perspective of the biblical teaching on covenant. Then we will see how this perspective is fruitful for an understanding of election and the priority of regeneration to faith in relation to the evangelistic task of the church. In the process, we will have to compare and contrast what may be called "election-evangelism," or "regeneration-evangelism," with what may be called "covenant-evangelism." Not all of the elements that will be mentioned as characteristics of election-evangelism and regeneration-evangelism will necessarily appear in the preaching of any one evangelist or pastor. However, they will be recognized as features that are generally character-istic of much of Reformed evangelism today.

If the evangelistic efforts of Reformed churches do not appear to have the impact that they ought to have, given our conviction that the Reformed faith is the best expression of biblical Christianity, we should not too hastily absolve ourselves from responsibility by saying that greater fruitful-ness apparently does not lie in the plan and purpose of God. That may well be true, of course. But it may also be true that we have failed to present the gospel from Reformed pulpits as genuinely good news for sinners, the good news of the grace of God for all people everywhere. The New Tes-tament represents the present age as one of unprecedented and superabundant blessing. Reformed churches ought to be experiencing that blessing in both the numerical and the spiritual growth of their congregations.

♋5

Covenant and the Great Commission

The Great Commission is found in Matthew 28:19–20. Jesus commands his disciples to "go and make disciples of all nations, baptizing them in the name of the Father and of the Son and of the Holy Spirit, and teaching them to obey everything I have commanded you." He adds this promise: "And surely I am with you always, to the very end of the age." The point here is that the Great Commission arises out of, and is patterned after, the covenant that God made with Abraham, as recorded in Genesis 17. We cannot properly understand what Jesus is telling his church to do except against this background.

The covenant made with Abraham entails both privilege and responsibility. Privilege comes to expression in the promises of the covenant. These include, first of all, the promise of a people. God promises Abraham, "I . . . will greatly increase your numbers" (v. 2). Indeed, Abraham will be "the father of many nations" (v. 4). Second, there is the promise of land. God promises to Abraham and his seed the land where he is now an alien for an everlasting possession (v. 8). This is the land of Canaan, the Promised Land. There is going to be both a people and a place for them to live. But just as there is more than one nation in view, so also is there more than one land in view. Ultimately, the land to be given to the multitude of nations as the people of God is the whole earth, the new heavens and the new earth. Therefore, the promise to Abraham also takes the form, "All peoples on earth will be blessed through you" (Gen. 12:3).

The heart of covenant privilege and blessing is expressed in the promise, "I will establish my covenant as an everlasting covenant between me and you and your descendants after you for the generations to come, to be your God and the God of your descendants after you" (Gen. 17:7). The heart of covenant privilege and blessing is union and communion with God.

Only with the advent of Jesus Christ, who is *the* seed of Abraham (Gal. 3:16), and by means of the Great Commission, do the covenant promises begin to be fulfilled on the grand scale in terms of which they were first given. Jesus commands his followers to make disciples of "all nations," so that in Christ, Abraham becomes the father of many nations. The Day of Pentecost marks the beginning of the worldwide spread of Christianity as representatives of the different nations from various parts of the world hear the gospel, each in his own language, and respond positively to it.

Because the promise to Abraham is a promise to his children as well, Peter promises the Holy Spirit both to "you and your children" (Acts 2:39). The promise of the Holy Spirit and the promise of Christ's abiding presence with his people are the initial fulfillment of the heart of covenant privilege and blessing, union and communion with God. When men "from every tribe and language and people and nation" have become "a kingdom and priests to serve our God" (Rev. 5:9–10), then the dwelling of God will, indeed, be with us. "God himself will be with them and be their God" (Rev. 21:3). The Great Commission is pregnant with the fulfillment of promise. Christ commissioned his church to see to it that the promises made to the fathers would be fulfilled, and the authority of the groom guarantees the fruitfulness of the bride.

At the same time, privilege entails responsibility. Abraham had to keep covenant with the Lord, as did his descendants to whom the promises were also made. The preeminent covenant keeper is Jesus Christ. He is *the* seed of Abraham, "obedient to death—even death on a cross" (Phil. 2:8). As the covenant is kept, according to the pattern of Jesus Christ, the promises of the covenant are fulfilled. This evangelistic methodology was spelled out to Abraham in precise terms: "For I have chosen him, so that he will direct his children and his household after him to keep the way of the LORD by doing what is right and just, so that the LORD will bring about for Abraham what he has promised him" (Gen. 18:19). Then "Abraham will surely become a great and powerful nation, and all nations on earth will be blessed through him" (v. 18).

Because the evangelistic methodology prescribed for Abraham and his descendants was to result in worldwide blessing, Jesus prescribed precisely the same methodology for his church when he said that all nations of the earth were to be discipled by "teaching them to obey everything I have commanded you" (Matt. 28:20). Just as the gospel of the Abrahamic covenant taught God's people to do what is right and just (Gen. 18:19), so the gospel of the new covenant teaches us to seek first the righteousness of the kingdom of God (Matt. 6:33). The gospel of the kingdom (Matt. 4:23) is the Sermon on the Mount (Matt. 5–7).

For Abraham, the sign of both covenant privilege and covenant responsibility was circumcision. Paul calls circumcision "a seal of the righteousness that he had by faith" (Rom. 4:11). The righteousness of faith is the obedience of faith (Rom. 1:5; 16:26), and is therefore simultaneously covenant privilege and responsibility.

Corresponding to circumcision in the Great Commission is baptism, indicative at once of the grace of God and the response of faith, repentance, and obedience. As the Israel of the old covenant becomes the church of the new covenant, the circumcised people of God must be baptized, as they were on the Day of Pentecost. At the same time, the circumcision of the nations is accomplished in and through their baptism into Christ. Circumcision was never merely, or even principally, a sign of national identity for the Jews. From the moment of its inception (Gen. 17), circumcision had preeminently multinational significance. Abraham and his children were to be circumcised because God promised that he would be the father not of one, but of many nations.

No more powerful argument for the transition from circumcision to baptism can be advanced than the correspondence between the covenant with Abraham, with its command to circumcise, and the commission of Christ, with its command to baptize.

It now becomes apparent why the New Testament opens with the repeated assertion that what was long before promised to Abraham is at last being brought to pass (Luke

1:55, 73). After the resurrection of Jesus from the dead, Peter and John understood that they were standing on the threshold of the ultimate fulfillment of this promise (Acts 3:25). Paul declares Abraham to be the father of believers under the new covenant because he understands their faith to be of a piece with that of Abraham (Rom. 4). As Paul and the other apostles evangelized in obedience to the Great Commission, they could see the promise to Abraham being fulfilled.

Throughout the Gospels and Acts, the Epistles, and on into Revelation, it is abundantly clear that the Great Commission arises out of, is patterned after, and must be understood in terms of, the covenant structure of the Old Testament. In particular, it must be understood in terms of the covenant made with Abraham. This means that if evangelistic methodology is developed in obedience to the Great Commission, it must be covenantal methodology. As such, it contrasts with methodologies oriented to the doctrines of election and regeneration.

∂6

Covenant and Election

Reformed evangelistic methodology must be consciously oriented to the doctrine of the covenant, rather than to the doctrine of election.

Arminianism developed out of Calvinism and as a reaction to it. Its evangelistic methodology is oriented to the particularistic doctrines of unconditional election, limited or definite atonement, irresistible grace, and perseverance of the saints, but in an entirely negative way. Arminians argue that God's election is based on his foresight of faith and that Christ died for all people. Every person is free to accept or reject his offer of pardon, and to do so repeatedly and ultimately. At the same time, the doctrine of total depravity is limited by our native ability to cooperate with the grace of God.

In this way, Arminians are initially quite successful in letting the gospel come across to modern man as good news. It is addressed to sinners individually and directly in the second person: "Christ loves you and has died for you.

What he has done for you is within your reach, not by much hard work, but by a simple act of faith. As long as you believe, you are forgiven and your decision is registered in the councils of eternity by God's election of you." This is good news. It would be a mistake on the part of the Reformed to deny that Arminian evangelism is often successful because such good news is appealing.

A more thorough analysis of the Arminian gospel reveals, however, that its good news is not as good as it could be, and for that reason is not good enough, or even good at all. What Christ has done for me needs to be supplemented by what I do for myself through faith and evangelical obedience. But salvation that is not wholly and exclusively of Christ is not salvation at all for totally depraved people. Therefore, Calvinists reject Arminianism and its characteristic evangelistic methodology.

For their part, Calvinists generally orient their evangelistic methodology to the five points, the particularistic doctrines that are the hallmark of the Reformed faith. God makes the ultimate decision concerning a person's destiny in his sovereign election before the foundation of the world. The more consistently this truth controls evangelism, the more consistently people both inside and outside the church are approached with the gospel as either elect or nonelect (reprobate). Some would go so far as to say that there is no good news in any sense for the reprobate. But if only the elect are effectually called to salvation, why does the gospel have to be preached to every person? The usual answer to this question is that "unfortunately" the evangelist does not know who the elect are. In order to call the elect effectually, everyone must hear the gospel. The idea seems to be that if the evangelist had insight into the decree of God and knew who the elect were, he would not have to waste his time with the reprobate.

Furthermore, since Christ has died only for particular persons (limited or definite atonement), whose identity can never be known with certainty, it is inconsistent with the Reformed faith to say to any specific person what Christ has done for him. This is certainly the case with respect to people outside the church of Christ, but it is also true to a large extent with respect to people inside the church. The pastor hesitates to cultivate a hearty assurance in this or that believer, because he does not know for certain whether that person is one of the elect and thus one for whom Christ died. His faith may prove to be temporary and his works hypocritical. To cultivate assurance under those circumstances would lead him away from the cross of Christ.

Because the Arminian has an accomplished redemption that is universal in scope though not effective for every person, he can apply it to particular individuals. Because the Calvinist has an accomplished redemption that is particular in scope though always effective for the elect, he cannot apply it to particular persons. The application has to be more general and abstract because he cannot distinguish between the elect and the reprobate in real life. That is why Reformed sermons on "the doctrines of sovereign grace" are often in the third person, expressed in terms of what Christ has done "for his own," or for those who "truly believe." The exception is the exploration of human sin, which can be, and often is, very specific and in the second person, because of the universality of sin and depravity.

It is now understandable why Calvinists tend to be more successful at preaching sin, condemnation, and death than at preaching the grace of our Lord Jesus Christ. This is the established, but dubious, reputation that they enjoy. They can be very pointed and specific with respect to sin, but not with respect to grace. Unlike Arminians, they have grace that is really and truly grace. Salvation from beginning to end, from conception in eternity to consummation in glory, is all of God and is summed up in the name of Jesus Christ. But they are hampered in getting that glorious gospel across to particular persons in the pew or on the street as *grace.*

The temptation is to compensate by emphasizing the personal application of the doctrines of sin, condemnation, and death, in the hope that the Holy Spirit will bring people to Christ, who is, in the context of preaching, held at a distance from them because of the doctrine of election. But the knowledge of sin is not in and of itself good news. It comes between the Redeemer and the sinner, obscuring the all-sufficiency of the Savior. However, the gospel tells us that Jesus comes between a sinner and his sin to save him from sin, condemnation, and death.

If the gospel does not come across to sinners as gospel, as genuinely good news, we cannot legitimately expect that multitudes will be saved. The frustration and ineffectiveness of many Reformed ministries may well be traced to precisely this point. The gospel alone brings life and immortality to light (2 Tim. 1:10), and it alone is the power of God for salvation (Rom. 1:16), yet it may not come across from Reformed pulpits in this way, as genuinely good news. If his evangelistic methodology is oriented to the doctrine of election, the Reformed pastor can at best wait, hope, and pray for occasional seasons of revival. But if his evangelistic methodology is consciously oriented to the Great Commission and God's gracious covenant, he can and ought to expect permanent vitality in the steady expansion of the church of Christ.

The answer to this theological dilemma, therefore, is not compromise with Arminianism, but the Reformed doctrine of the covenant. The Bible itself, and the New Testament in particular, provide the data that give rise to the dilemma, and yet there is no consciousness of it in the Bible itself. Faith and salvation come only by the predestinating grace of God to particular persons. Surely the angel of the Lord knew this when he came to the shepherds near Bethlehem and said, "Do not be afraid. I bring you *good news* of great joy that will be *for all the people*" (Luke 2:10).

The reason why the Bible is not conscious of this dilemma is not that the prophets and apostles who wrote it were not as intellectually or theologically sharp as we are. Rather, the reason is that *the prophets and apostles viewed election from the perspective of the covenant,* whereas we have tended to view the covenant from the perspective of election.

From the perspective of the covenant, there is mystery because we are creatures and God is the Creator. We cannot know God exhaustively. God remains incomprehensible. We can never know God's decree as he knows it, and for that reason we cannot begin to reflect on his salvation from the perspective of the decree, even though our salvation originates in the predestinating love and purpose of God. To look at covenant from the perspective of election is ultimately to yield to the primal temptation to be as God. The proper stance for Adam and for all of us after him is a covenantal stance of faithful obedience. Only from that perspective can election be understood as grace. Therefore, although from the perspective of covenant there is mystery, there is no dilemma and no paradox or contradiction.

Evangelism, when patterned according to the Great

Commission and the covenant, does not address people as a mixed multitude of elect and reprobate, with a view toward separating them. Evangelism addresses people as covenant breakers in rebellion against God and opens up to them covenant life in union and communion with God. It points us to the finished work of Christ. In utter sincerity and without equivocation, Reformed evangelism calls every person to life in the way of faith, repentance, and obedience, with the assurance that Jesus will not refuse anyone who cries out to him for mercy. The evangelist labors in the confidence that God really stands behind the message that he has authorized him to preach to all people. God has wrought a finished and complete redemption, and so salvation (and not merely the possibility of salvation) is offered sincerely and without equivocation to all. "For God so loved the world that he gave his one and only Son, that whoever believes in him shall not perish but have eternal life" (John 3:16).

When the Arminian comes to this verse, which expresses the essence of the gospel, he finds it necessary to hedge on the absolute sufficiency of the atonement. Because the atonement is universal, made for all people and not just the elect, it is not really effective unless it is made so by an act of faith on the part of the sinner. On his part, the Calvinist frequently hedges on the extent of the world, because the saving love of God revealed in the atonement is only for the elect. Both the Arminian and the Calvinist look at John 3:16 in terms of the doctrine of election, the one denying it and the other upholding it. From the perspective of the covenant, however, all of the words of John 3:16 mean exactly what they say.

The Reformed evangelist can and must preach to everyone on the basis of John 3:16, "Christ died to save you." The death of Christ is inherently efficacious; otherwise, it would not be gracious. The world is the world of human beings blinded and crippled by Satan, the prince of this world. Christ did not die for inanimate objects or preternatural beings, nor did he die for abstractions. He died for people, for sinners, for you and for me.

If we look at this message, "Christ died to save you," from the perspective of election, it is only possibly true, and may well be false. From this perspective, Christ died only for the elect and not for the reprobate. But John 3:16 is embedded in the covenant documents of the New Testament. As such, it is not an elaboration of the doctrine of election or a commentary on the extent of the atonement. Rather, John 3:16 is covenant truth. Its specific application—and this is what the proclamation of the gospel must be—in the declaration, "Christ died for you," is a demonstration of the grace of our Lord Jesus Christ opening the way to fellowship with God.

As such, it calls each and every sinner to that fellowship, but not on the assumption that people have the native ability to believe, contrary to the doctrine of total depravity. Rather, it calls sinners to fellowship with God because God has brought his salvation near in the person of Jesus Christ and has made it accessible to us. Paul argues in Romans 3:25 that sins committed under the old covenant were left unpunished. But now Jesus has come and made atonement for sin. He has atoned not only for the sins of the Jews, but for the sins of the whole world. We command sinners to believe in Jesus, not because we think that they have the native ability to believe, but because only by believing can they be saved and have eternal life. By demanding faith and repentance, the gospel does not throw us back on our own resources, but brings us eyeball-to-eyeball with Jesus Christ, who alone is the Way, the Truth, and the Life.

By the grace and gift of God, sinners do receive and accept Jesus Christ as Lord and Savior. Now as they look at their experience from the perspective of their covenant fellowship with God in Christ through the indwelling Spirit, they confess that they are where they are wholly and exclusively because of the electing grace of God. The order of the apostolic benediction is not without theological significance: "May the grace of the Lord Jesus Christ, and the love of God, and the fellowship of the Holy Spirit be with you all" (2 Cor. 13:14). The benediction begins with the grace of the Lord Jesus Christ because it is only in terms of covenant grace that we can know the electing love of God from eternity and be assured of the communion of the Holy Spirit for eternity.

This all-pervasive covenant perspective on the church and its work is evident on every page of Scripture. Two passages will serve to illuminate that perspective and indicate how it helps us come to grips with what are sometimes considered exegetical problems. Often what a passage says is clear enough so that the problem is not really exegetical. The problem arises when we try to incorporate what the passage obviously intends to say into our theology.

The first passage is Ephesians 1:1–14. These verses are suffused with covenantal language. The Ephesians are a congregation of the Lord Jesus Christ, enjoying the spiritual blessings of sanctity of life, adoption to sonship, forgiveness of sins, and the seal of the Holy Spirit. At the same time, all of these blessings are traced back to the predestinating love of God. This accent comes through so strongly and so repeatedly at the very beginning of the letter, that Paul may even appear to be writing from the perspective of election. We would then have to understand his letter from that perspective. We would have to look at the covenant in the light of election.

Careful attention to the language of these verses makes clear, however, that precisely the reverse is the case. Paul looks at election from the perspective of covenant. For that reason, predestination is not a theological puzzle, but a cause for gratitude. When Paul says, "He chose us" (v. 4), we must ask who "we" are. We could say that they are the saints in Ephesus and the faithful in Christ Jesus (v. 1), and that because he was an organ of revelation, he knew that each and every member of that congregation was eternally elect of God. Grammatically and even theoretically, such an interpretation is possible. But it is utterly artificial, especially in view of the serious problems that Paul had to contend with in the churches he founded.

One could also argue that there were nonelect people in the congregation, but that the letter does not address them. Again, this is grammatically and theoretically possible. But are we to think that Paul was addressing only some of those on the roll of the Ephesian church and had nothing to say to the rest? How would these people know who they were?

Any attempt to understand Paul's statement, "He chose us," as though Paul had direct insight into the eternal decree of God, is bound to be both artificial and impractical. No pastor or evangelist could use that language today because we don't know who the elect are.

In Ephesians 1, Paul writes from the perspective of observable covenant reality and concludes from the visible faith and sanctity of the Ephesians that they are the elect of

God. He addresses them as such and encourages them to think of themselves as elect. A Reformed pastor can and must do the same today. He has the great joy and delight of publicly acknowledging the work that the Holy Spirit is doing in the lives of the people to whom he is ministering. Hebrews 6:10 says that "God is not unjust; he will not forget your work and the love you have shown him as you have helped his people and continue to help them." If God is not unjust, then the Reformed pastor ought not to be unjust either. If we are unjust, we are in danger of losing the gospel. Injustice is not good news.

It is true that some in the congregation may fall away and leave the church. Paul issues a warning in view of that possibility. Were some to fall away, he would no longer speak of them as the elect of God. However, he would not confess that "unfortunately" his initial judgment had been wrong. There is nothing unfortunate about the fact that we do not have insight into the eternal decree of God and therefore cannot make infallible judgments about the elect or reprobate state of people. It would be most unfortunate if we could, for we would then have succeeded in destroying God by becoming the same as God. Paul is right to address the saints and faithful in Ephesus as elect, and at the same time he is right to warn them against apostasy. He has the freedom to do this and senses no dilemma in doing so, because he has evangelized the Ephesians using a covenant methodology in accordance with the Great Commission. Only by following the same methodology can the Reformed pastor today enjoy the Pauline freedom to speak grace and encouragement to the flesh-and-blood people seated before him in his congregation.

A second passage that is illustrative of the covenant per-

spective on election is John 15:1–8. Jesus is clearly and un-
ambiguously saying in this passage that he is the vine and
that his hearers are branches abiding in him. He exhorts
them all to continue abiding in him by bearing fruit, and
that means by persevering in faith and obedience. If they
do, the Father will see to it that they bear even more fruit.
They are at no point cast upon their own resources, because
as branches they get their vitality at every point from the
vine. On the other hand, if certain branches do not abide in
Christ, but deny him and become disobedient, the Father
will cut them off and destroy them. The passage is a grand
exhortation to covenant faithfulness, enveloped in the over-
flowing grace of Christ.

Frequently, however, this passage has created nothing
but problems. Often the first question (and sometimes the
only question) asked is, "How can this passage be squared
with the doctrines of election and the perseverance of the
saints?" The answer begins with an explanation of what the
passage cannot mean in the light of these doctrines. The
question is then resolved by distinguishing between two
kinds of branches. Some branches are not really in Christ in
a saving way. They are in him only "outwardly," and what-
ever fruit there is, is not genuine. These branches are even-
tually cut off and destroyed. Other branches are truly
branches. They are in Christ "inwardly" or savingly. They
bear more and more fruit as they are pruned and cultivated
by the Father.

If this distinction is in the text, it is difficult to see what
the point of the warning is. The outward branches cannot
profit from it, because they cannot in any case bear genuine
fruit. They are not related to Christ inwardly and draw no
life from him. The inward branches do not need the warn-

ing, because they are vitalized by Christ and therefore cannot help but bear good fruit. Cultivation by the Father, with its attendant blessing, is guaranteed.

The words *inward* and *outward* are often used in Reformed theology to resolve problems that arise because biblical texts are approached from the perspective of election. Indeed, the seeming indispensability of this formula indicates that the covenant is commonly viewed from the perspective of election, rather than election from the perspective of covenant. The distinction is necessary to account for the fact that the covenant community appears to include both elect and nonelect. The nonelect are then said to be only outwardly in the covenant. The elect are inwardly in the covenant. Covenant is virtually dissolved into the idea of election.

The terms *outwardly* and *inwardly* are biblical terms, but when Paul uses them in Romans 2:28–29, he is not referring to the *elect* and the *reprobate*. The terms describe the difference between covenantally loyal Jews and disobedient transgressors of the law. The categories derive their meaning from the covenant, not from the decree.

Ephesians 1:1–14, John 15:1–8, and similar passages can be understood properly only within the context of the covenant. In Deuteronomy, the great covenant document of the Old Testament, Moses writes, "The secret things belong to the LORD our God, but the things revealed belong to us and to our children forever, that we may follow all the words of this law" (Deut. 29:29). This verse means more than that we do not know who the elect are. It means that we cannot conduct our affairs as though we were God. We have to live as creatures made by God to live by the light of his word. The application of this principle to evangelism means that a Reformed methodology must be oriented to the doctrine of the covenant, rather than to the doctrine of election. In light of the covenant, we learn that the particularistic doctrines of Calvinism are pure grace and not a mixture of blessing and curse.

ॐ7

Covenant and Regeneration

When Reformed evangelism is oriented to the doctrine of election, it is only a logical and natural extension of this method to orient evangelism also to regeneration. Regeneration is the new birth, the initial transformation of a sinner wrought by the Holy Spirit. The Holy Spirit renews the sinner in the innermost core of his being so that he can repent of sin and believe the gospel. Regeneration comes before faith, and unless a sinner who is dead in transgressions and sins is made alive by being born again, he cannot believe the gospel and be saved. Regeneration is a secret operation of the Spirit, and through it the Spirit begins to apply to the elect what was granted to them in the secret counsel of God. In evangelism, therefore, the relationship between regeneration and covenant is similar to the relationship between election and covenant. If evangelism is oriented to regeneration, the covenant is again viewed from the perspective of a secret work of God—now from the perspective of regeneration.

But instead of looking at covenant from the perspective of regeneration, we ought to look at regeneration from the perspective of covenant. When that happens, baptism, the sign and seal of the covenant, marks the point of conversion. Baptism is the moment when we see the transition from death to life and a person is saved.

This is not to say that baptism accomplishes the transition from death to life, or that baptism causes a person to be born again. That is the doctrine of baptismal regeneration, which is rightly rejected by Reformed churches. The Holy Spirit works where, when, and how he pleases, not necessarily at the precise moment of baptism.

From the perspective of election, regeneration is the point of conversion. Regeneration, however, is a secret work of the Holy Spirit, and so we do not know when it takes place. We do not have access to the moment of regeneration. What we hear from the converted sinner is a profession of faith, and what we see is his baptism into Christ. This covenant sign and seal marks his conversion and his entrance into the church as the body of Christ. From the perspective of the covenant, he is united to Christ when he is baptized.

When evangelism is oriented to regeneration as the point of transition, rather than to baptism as the mark of transition, it is necessary for the evangelist or pastor to begin by making some kind of judgment with respect to the spiritual condition of those whom he is addressing. If they are perceived to be regenerate, there is no need to say things that would lead to their regeneration. These people must be addressed differently from those who are not perceived to be regenerate and from whom the fruits of regeneration cannot be expected. Since most congregations are made up of both regenerate and unregenerate people, there is often a twofold application of the message, one to the converted and another to the unconverted. Some argue that since a false sense of security is most dangerous to the welfare of souls, it is best to assume that all hearers are in an unregenerate state. This would amount to a doctrine of presumptive nonregeneration. That is the opposite of presumptive regeneration, which teaches that all the members of the congregation, including baptized infants, are to be regarded as born again, unless and until they show by their words or deeds that they are not regenerate. In any case, whether the congregation is thought of as regenerate, unregenerate, or a mixed multitude, a judgment is made concerning their regenerate state either expressly or by implication.

With respect to a congregation as a whole, the judgment has to be more general, but in personal evangelism it can be quite specific. Whether the evangelist thinks of his conversation partner as regenerate or not will determine the character of their encounter. In counseling a church member who has fallen into some grievous sin, the pastor may suggest that the root problem lies in the fact that the counselee has not been born again. In informal conversation among Reformed Christians, one often hears the opinion expressed that a certain person is or is not "really converted." These judgments are usually made, to be sure, with allowance for a margin of error. We recognize that God is the ultimate and only infallible judge. Therefore, in the case of a brother or sister who is thought to be regenerate, but who departs from the faith, the previous estimate has to be revised to say that in all probability the brother or sister is not regenerate after all.

Problems with the method of regeneration-evangelism emerge right at the start. Judgments have to be made that belong properly and exclusively in the hands of God. No person can judge the heart of another person. To presume to do so is to yield again to the primal temptation to be as God. This objection is valid even when a judgment is hedged by the acknowledgment that final judgment belongs to God, and that what is attempted is only an approximation of God's judgment. No one should even attempt to approximate God's judgment. To do so will only lead to frustration in ministry. Numerous Reformed pastors have undoubtedly been discouraged in evangelism because they have thought of themselves as lacking the ability to judge human hearts. Again, the operative principle must be that the secret things belong to the Lord our God. When Jesus spoke of the new birth and compared the Spirit's operation to the wind (John 3:8), he made clear that regeneration is a secret work of God and therefore cannot be used by us as a point of orientation for evangelism.

However, once the judgment is made that a given person is unregenerate and therefore a candidate for evangelism, the evangelist adopts a procedure to secure his regeneration. Regeneration is, of course, the immediate, internal work of the Spirit. Therefore, the evangelist does not actually cause his hearer to be regenerated. Nevertheless, he tries to lead his hearer to the very threshold of regeneration. Evangelism becomes preparation for regeneration.

One way to prepare the sinner for conversion is to lay great emphasis upon the demands of the law. Over against methods that ask the hearer simply to believe the message or to believe in Jesus ("easy believism"), Reformed evangelists will stress that God does not simply require faith in the narrow sense of an act of trust, but also obedience to the law at every point. However, it becomes apparent sooner or later that although the evangelist asks for obedience, he does not really expect it; indeed, he would consider himself a failure if the obedience, or an attempt at it, were forthcoming. That would amount to an impossible attempt at salvation by works. The real intent of preaching the law (as distinct from preaching Christ or the gospel) is to demonstrate that the hearer *cannot* obey it. In fact, he is shown to be hopelessly entangled in innumerable transgressions of the law, stemming from a heart that is hostile toward God and needs to be regenerated.

After the law has done its work of convicting the sinner, so that he is utterly humbled before the wrath of God, or sometimes along with this preaching of law, Jesus is held forth as the one who offers forgiveness on the basis of his death on the cross. He will grant repentance from sin as well as new obedience. Jesus can be grasped only by faith, and the listener is told to believe and to repent of his sin. At the same time, he is told that he cannot believe or repent any more than he can obey. A new heart is necessary. The climax of the gospel appeal is reached when the hearer is urged to ask God for a new heart with which to lay hold of the grace of Christ.

If the Lord is pleased to regenerate the hearer, the new heart, which is in itself invisible, begins to show itself at once in the exercise of faith, repentance, and new obedience. The new convert will usually confess his faith publicly after a period of instruction and may then be baptized, if not already baptized (or if the previous baptism is regarded as invalid).

While there are obvious biblical motifs evidenced in this preparatory phase, there are also serious questions that have to be raised. For example, if regeneration is the work of the

Holy Spirit, does not a method of evangelism geared to result in regeneration and the evoking of a corresponding crisis experience begin to encroach upon the work of the Spirit? To labor for a specific result that is beyond the pastor's power to bring forth can be frustrating, if not even paralyzing.

Furthermore, a serious tension is set up between the demand for faith and repentance, on the one hand, and the denial of any ability to do what is demanded, on the other. The tension is all too familiar to any Reformed pastor who has sought to work out an evangelistic method consistent with his principles. Even the exhortation to ask for a new heart does not square with the doctrine of total inability. There is *nothing* the unregenerate person can do or will do to move toward conversion. At the same time, although Christ is made visible, he is still held at a distance and out of the reach of the sinner. The fact that God does regenerate and save people in connection with this methodology has little or nothing to do with what is said in the evangelistic message. The message tells the sinner that he cannot do what he must do, and describes what might happen in a given case. But it is difficult to see how a message that focuses on the inability of the sinner to respond, and therefore holds Christ at a distance, will come across to him as good news. At best, it would appear to be a mixed message. It may not be far amiss to suggest that some otherwise able and conscientious evangelists and pastors have abandoned the ministry rather than live with this tension.

Once the crisis of regeneration is passed, however, and begins to register itself in faith, repentance, and obedience, the law is once again at the center as the rule of obedience. If regeneration is seen as the preeminent work of grace and therefore the very essence of salvation, subsequent law keeping will tend to savor of works-righteousness supplementing this work of grace. This danger is avoided by referring to the indwelling Spirit as the source of the new obedience. Works done in faith often continue to be oriented to regeneration, in that they are prized mainly for their evidential value. They prove that regeneration, and thus salvation, has really and truly taken place.

The difficulty here is that new obedience is often represented from the pulpit as being so minimal and sin so prevailing in the lives of those who are converted, that one is compelled to ask whether there is all that much difference between regenerate and unregenerate people. The work of grace has been done and the sinner has received a new heart, but the graciousness of it all will appear only at death, when he will be perfectly sanctified. If the same passages of Scripture are used to describe human sinfulness both before and after regeneration, it is difficult to see how the grace of our Lord Jesus Christ is gracious here and now.

In addition, if the new obedience is minimal, so also is the assurance of faith and the joy in salvation that is to be generated through self-examination. Indeed, even those works that provide evidence of new life may themselves be deceptive and hypocritical. Therefore, it becomes necessary to monitor one's assumed regeneration constantly. The anxiety of the believer under this kind of instruction bears a marked resemblance to the anxiety of Martin Luther that caused him so much grief prior to his discovery of the grace of God. Now the problem is not salvation by works, but assurance by works.

Moreover, regeneration-evangelism tends to focus on the person and his experience. This has sometimes led to elaborate descriptions of the steps leading to regeneration and the subsequent marks of regeneration in an attempt to ascertain the genuineness of the crisis experience itself. In line with this is the attention given to the experiences of other people as patterns for our own experience, or as encouragement to think that what has happened to others can happen to me as well. It is not altogether inconceivable that in the experiences of other believers, the Christ who is held at a distance in preaching is made incarnate and brought near. Probably for this reason, some evangelists suppose that their experience-centered preaching is actually Christ-centered preaching. Especially gifted evangelists also run the risk of becoming Christ figures. Even in Reformed circles, it has not been superfluous to warn against attachment to the man, and to urge attachment to the message and to the Christ of whom the message speaks.

In contrast to regeneration-evangelism, a methodology oriented to the covenant structure of Scripture and to the Great Commission presents baptism as the transition point from death to life. The specific terms of the Great Commission describe the process of making disciples in terms of baptism and instruction in the commands of Christ. This means that evangelism does not end with regeneration, but continues as long as a person lives. Baptism marks the entrance into the kingdom of God and the beginning of life-long training as kingdom subjects. According to the Great Commission, conversion without baptism is an anomaly. A sinner is not "really converted" until he is baptized.

The orientation of evangelism to regeneration tends to discount the significance of baptism as marking the point of transition. Either it comes too early, as in the case of infant baptism, so that one cannot say for sure whether the child is regenerate, or else it comes too late, as a kind of appendix to the crisis experience of conversion. Even in Reformed circles, it is common to speak of the number of persons who are "really converted" or "truly Christian," although the Bible itself avoids such language and talks in terms of the number of people baptized. The three thousand souls added to the church on the Day of Pentecost are described as having been baptized (Acts 2:41). The Philippian jailer and the members of his household are not said to have been regenerated or converted, but baptized (Acts 16:33). Paul's experience on the road to Damascus is usually thought of as the time of his conversion. The Bible does not say when he was regenerated, but it does say when he was baptized (Acts 9:18). His baptism marks the time when his sins were washed away (Acts 22:16). When Paul exhorts the Romans to obey God, he does not remind them that they were regenerated or suggest that they might not be regenerate. Rather, he points to their baptism and calls them to live out of that experience (Rom. 6:1–11).

Since regeneration is one of the secret things that belong to God, the evangelists in Scripture do not presume to have access to knowledge of it in individual cases. They govern the church in terms of what is open and obvious to all. Christians are those who have been baptized. Unbelievers are those who have not been baptized. In our day, this pattern is usually more evident in parts of the world where baptized Christians are in a distinct minority. Where church members suffer social alienation and ostracism because of their faith, baptism marks the moment of transition when believers take a public stand for Christ. There are no secret believers, but only baptized believers.

Why does baptism play such a minor role in modern evangelistic methodology, when it holds the major place in the Great Commission? The reason would appear to lie in the preference for regeneration-evangelism over covenant-evangelism. But when regeneration is understood from the perspective of covenant, it becomes both clear and natural that baptism, as the sign of the covenant, should mark the passage from death to life. It did just that in the experience of Jesus Christ, the head of the new covenant. That is, the death of Jesus and his subsequent resurrection are described as a baptism (Mark 10:38; Luke 12:50). His baptism meant that old things had passed away and all things had become new. The same is true for the baptized believer, at least in principle. The baptism of the believer marks his identification with Christ in death and resurrection, and therefore his own passage from death to life.

The covenantal focus on baptism does not mean that regeneration is discounted. Rather, the new birth is put in proper perspective. The connection between baptism and regeneration comes to vivid expression when Paul says that we are saved "through the washing of rebirth and renewal by the Holy Spirit" (Titus 3:5). He also says that we are washed, sanctified, and justified in the name of the Lord Jesus Christ and by the Spirit of God (1 Cor. 6:11). A comparison of the forms of the Great Commission in Matthew and Luke (Matt. 28:19 and Luke 24:47) shows the correlation of baptism, repentance, and remission of sins. Baptism is therefore to be understood as of a piece with the total transformation that is salvation. It is the sacramental side of the total renewal (regeneration in the broad sense) of both the inner and the outer man.

What leads to baptism, according to Luke's version of the Great Commission, is the proclamation of repentance and remission of sin. This follows the pattern set by John the Baptist. John proclaimed repentance and remission of sin, leading to baptism—and even to the baptism of Jesus in the Jordan River. His prophetic ministry, viewed as a whole, led to the baptism of Jesus on the cross. Evangelistic preaching teaches us that there is life only in fellowship with the living God and warns us that by nature we are not only out of fellowship with God, but in rebellion against him. Rebellion issues in destruction and death, but Jesus, the God of our salvation, has come to die for us, so that we do not have to die. He lives again, so that we, too, can live in him. Because he has come, salvation is near. This is the good news. Jesus calls us to follow him in faith, repentance, and obedience. Paul says, "We are bringing you good news, telling you to turn from these worthless things to the living God, who made heaven and earth and sea and everything in them" (Acts 14:15). To turn from sin in penitent obedience is to be free from sin. Jesus died, not merely to save us from death at the final judgment, but to save us from sin now, and that is good news.

We can lay hold of Christ and be saved. This good news is going to be misunderstood, as it was by the Pharisees of Christ's day and by their cohorts ever since, in terms of native ability and meritorious works-righteousness. But any attempt to counter the error by accenting total depravity and passive waiting for regeneration will only perpetuate the error by turning it inside out. Paul counters works with grace. He counters sinful inaction with divine action that requires a response. "He saved us, not because of righteous things we had done, but because of his mercy. He saved us through the washing of rebirth and renewal by the Holy Spirit" (Titus 3:5). "And now what are you waiting for? Get up, be baptized and wash your sins away, calling on his name" (Acts 22:16).

It now becomes apparent why baptism is coupled in the Great Commission with instruction in obedience to the commands of Christ. The sins that are washed away in baptism are supplanted by the righteousness of the kingdom of God. Sin is not only dethroned, but destroyed. Instruction in righteousness binds us to Christ, who is our righteousness and sanctification (1 Cor. 1:30). Christ, who obeyed the law for us, is obedient in us. The words of the law "are not just idle words for you—they are your life" (Deut. 32:47), because Christ is the Way, the Truth, and the Life (John 14:6).

It is both striking and significant that the Great Commission in neither Matthew nor Luke speaks of calling upon sinners to believe. Faith is not mentioned specifically, but only by implication. What is explicitly asserted is the call to repentance and obedience. When the call to faith is isolated from the call to obedience, as it frequently is, the effect is to make good works a supplement to salvation or simply the evidence of salvation. Some would even make them an optional supplement. According to the Great Commission, however, they belong to the essence of salvation, which is freedom from sin and not simply freedom from eternal condemnation as the consequence of sin. Because good works are done in obedience to all that Christ has commanded, they are suffused with and qualified by faith, without which no one can please God (Heb. 11:6).

All who have been baptized and are seeking in faith to do the will of God are to be regarded as Christian brothers and sisters. There are those who are going to stumble along the way, but the goal of instruction and discipline is to form a people of God who do not stumble. When the Lord led Israel out of Egypt, "from among their tribes no one faltered"

(Ps. 105:37). Large portions of the letters in the New Testament consist of instruction to wayward and stumbling church members. Discipline does not begin with mental excommunication ("He is not regenerate and never was one of us"), followed by verbal scolding and eventual neglect. Discipline, like discipling, is a matter of teaching and encouraging one's brother to observe all that Christ has commanded, in view of the hope that is laid up for all who love Christ and keep his commandments.

If the brother persists in sin, then he must be excommunicated, not by subtle innuendo from the pulpit, but by removal from the membership roll of the congregation. Until a process of discipline has been carried to that point, the brother must continue to be regarded and treated as a brother in Christ. This is not some condescending "judgment of charity," but a right the brother has because of his baptism. The good news is that Christ heals the stumbling cripples and makes the helplessly blind to see.

Covenant-evangelism guarantees that the gospel is and continues to be genuinely good news. Good Calvinists can and ought to be good evangelists. They have the freedom to declare that salvation rests wholly and exclusively on God's love in Christ from before the foundation of the world, according to his sovereign, electing purpose. At the same time, they have the freedom to call every sinner to surrender to Christ in faith for salvation and eternal life. We plead with sinners to come to Jesus, not because we believe they have the native ability to do so, but because Jesus is the only Savior. We believe that "he is able to save completely those who come to God through him, because he always lives to intercede for them" (Heb. 7:25).

Index of Scripture